F-15
EAGLE AT WAR

F-15
EAGLE AT WAR

TYSON V. RININGER

ZENITH PRESS

To my Grandmother
You always wished the best for me and looked forward to the completion of each new project.
How I wish you were here to see this as well. Miss you much.
Your grandson

First published in 2009 by Zenith Press, an imprint of MBI Publishing Company, 400 1st Avenue North, Suite 300, Minneapolis, MN 55401 USA.

Zenith Press titles are also available at discounts in bulk quantity for industrial or sales-promotional use. For details write to Special Sales Manager at MBI Publishing Company, 400 1st Avenue North, Suite 300, Minneapolis, MN 55401 USA.

To find out more about our books, join us online at www.zenithpress.com.

Library of Congress Cataloging-in-Publication Data

Rininger, Tyson V., 1974–
    F-15 Eagle at war / Tyson V. Rininger.
       p. cm.
    Includes index.
    ISBN 978-0-7603-3350-1 (sb : alk. paper)
    1. Eagle (Jet fighter plane) 2. Airplanes, Military—United States. I. Title.
    UG1242.F5R56 2009
    623.74'64—dc22
                            2008023066

On the cover, main: With fewer government threats and sufficient, current technology, the F-15 may survive longer than predicted. Furthermore, cost versus performance evaluation of the new F-22 Raptor found the aircraft insufficient and orders for F-22s were cut in half. This forced a number of F-15s to remain in service for many years to come. *Tyson V. Rininger*

Inset: Originally operated by the 53rd Tactical Fighter Squadron based at Bitburg, Germany, this Eagle was one of two flown on a historic sortie, February 6, 1991. Captain Thomas Dietz, flying airframe 79-0078 (pictured), and Lt. Bob Hehemann, in Eagle 84-0019, shot down two aircraft each during Operation Desert Storm. Dietz shot down two MiG-21s while Hehemann downed two Su-25s. The aircraft currently serves with the 58th Fighter Squadron at Eglin Air Force Base, Florida. *USAF*

On the frontispiece: Freshly painted Eagles from the 18th Tactical Fighter Wing adorn the flight line at Kadena Air Base in Japan. Maintenance personnel and flight crews preflight some of the squadron's F-15s during exercise Giant Warrior 1989. *USAF*

On the title page: A Strike Eagle from the 335th Fighter Squadron based at Seymour-Johnson Air Force Base returns from a Red Flag mission. *Tyson V. Rininger*

On the back cover: The F-15's design provided for an assortment of weaponry. This Eagle shows off its four square-finned AIM-9 Sidewinders along with the four additional triangle-finned AIM-7 Sparrows. *USAF*

About the author

Tyson V. Rininger has worked as a professional photographer for nearly twenty years, beginning his career while still in high school. His books include *Red Flag: Air Combat for the 21st Century* and *The Art of Flight,* and his photos and articles are routinely published in numerous high-profile magazines. When not hanging out of airplanes, he can be found working with various automotive, corporate, and studio clientele including the Monterey Bay Aquarium and the Western States Horse Expo. As a resident of Monterey, California, he volunteers his time working as the photographer and promotional materials designer for the California International Airshow in nearby Salinas. Recently he joined forces with Ken James and Mike Fox to create White Fox Media in an effort to assist corporations in achieving global image distribution for more affective marketing.

Editor: Steve Gansen
Designer: Danielle Smith

Printed in Singapore

CONTENTS

The Eagle has reigned supreme for more than thirty-five years. To this day, despite more than one hundred kills, not a single F-15 has been lost to a hostile adversary. *USAF*

CHAPTER ONE

F-15 CONCEPT

WITH ITS EDGY YET GRACEFUL LINES, THE world's greatest air superiority fighter of all time took to the skies in July 1972. It changed the history of aerial combat and the meaning of air supremacy forever. Shattering speed records and climbing to altitudes never before thought attainable for a fighter its size, the McDonnell Douglas F-15 Eagle has been the U.S. Air Force's (USAF) premier strike fighter for more than thirty-five years.

The F-15 combines superb aerodynamics with improved acceleration along with advanced avionics and aerial weaponry, making it a formidable adversary. However, getting to this point was not an overnight accomplishment.

The U.S. reached the pinnacle of air superiority during World War II with the incredible P-51 Mustang. Shortly following the war, radar and avionics technology had improved to the point where American forces felt there would no longer be a need for aircraft capable of air-to-air combat.

During the Korean War, American and allied forces faced their first real aerial battles against fighters of the Union of Soviet Socialist Republics (USSR), namely the agile, single-engine, swept-wing Mikoyan-Gurevich-designed MiG-15. The North American Treaty Organization (NATO) designated the Soviet plane "Fagot." The MiG proved a worthy adversary against straight-winged fighters like the P-80 and Britain's Gloster Meteor, along with World War II veterans like the F-4U Corsair and F-51 Mustang.

In 1949, the North American F-86 Sabre entered service with the USAF. It was the result of the Navy's

One of the most successful aerial fighters, the P-51 Mustang ruled the skies during World War II. Although dogfighting and close-quarter aerial combat was later considered obsolete, knowledge from flying aircraft like the P-51 helped regain aerial supremacy. *Tyson V. Rininger*

FJ program's request for a swept-wing carrier-based fighter. With the MiG-15's introduction to the skies over Korea in 1950, the USAF dispatched three F-86 squadrons in an attempt to maintain the upper hand. The Sabre was more agile than the MiG when it came to turning and diving, but the MiG was able to outdo the American fighter in rate of climb, acceleration, and ceiling. Fortunately, pilots of the F-86 were well-versed at aerial combat. Many had flown multiple missions during World War II.

Despite the experience of U.S. pilots, Soviet forces sent along accomplished pilots and instructors intimately familiar with the MiG's characteristics. This helped even the playing field and exposed weaknesses in the F-86.

On September 21, 1953, Lt. Kum Sok No, a twenty-one-year-old North Korean Air Force MiG pilot, defected to Kimpo Air Force Base in Seoul, Korea. Before the day's end, the aircraft was crated and shipped to Okinawa on its way to the U.S. One of the test pilots, Charles E. "Chuck" Yeager, put the MiG-15 through its paces over Muroc Dry Lake, now known as Edwards Air Force Base. Even though the aircraft proved to be an incredible advancement in aerodynamics and maneuverability due to its simplicity, trials at Muroc unveiled weaknesses that could be overcome. The creation of the North American F-86E Sabre and its all-moving tailplane improved maneuverability enough to maintain the upper hand over the Soviet aircraft. The USAF originally showed kill ratios as high as 10:1 favoring the F-86. After multiple studies and discrepancies, ratios of 4:1 and as low as 2:1 seemed closer to reality.

While touting higher than accurate success rates, the U.S. found itself involved in the Vietnam War. During this period, the Strategic Air Command (SAC) played a large role in the USAF operation. It felt that all aircraft needed to fulfill the role of nuclear weapons delivery. With this notion, air-to-air conflicts were thought of as a thing of the past. Strategic Air

During the Korean and Vietnam Wars, the MiG-15 and MiG-17 dominated the skies. The USAF considered dogfighting a thing of the past. The Strategic Air Command (SAC) planned future air development around long-range bombing tactics, intercontinental ballistic missile systems (ICBM), and high-altitude bombing runs. The Soviet-developed MiGs ensured that dogfighting remained a common tactic. *Tyson V. Rininger*

Lieutenant Kum Sok No of North Korea defected to Kimpo Air Force Base on September 21, 1953. This photograph shows his MiG-15 guarded by air police at a U.S. Air Force installation on Okinawa. Later testing of the MiG enabled American pilots to learn the enemy's weak points and became the basis of the F-86 Sabre. *USAF*

Command's push to create multi-role fighters, such as the Century Series and the F-4 Phantom, allowed adversary forces to control the skies. Communist air forces took advantage of the lessons learned with the MiG-15 and created the more agile and faster MiG-17, MiG-19, and MiG-21.

With the need for ground support over the Vietnam jungles, American aircraft were laden with bombs. Air superiority no longer took precedence. The simple, yet effective, tactic for communist air forces was to intercept the American fighters, force them to prematurely drop their payload, and proceed to engage in aerial combat. Few American fighters were equipped with precision guns. Their only form of air-to-air weapons were early-model AIM-7 Sparrows and AIM-9 Sidewinders that were intended to engage larger bombers. They were ineffective against the more nimble aircraft. Once those options had been exhausted, there were no alternatives. Intercept aircraft such as the F-102, F-104, and F-106 were unable to assist due to their lack of close support weaponry and inefficient maneuvering abilities. Allied airforce kill ratios plummeted to a disappointing 1:1. At times, even lower numbers resulted.

Although the North American F-100 Super Sabre was the first aircraft capable of exceeding the speed

Development of the F-86 Sabre was in direct response to the threats of the MiG-15 and MiG-17. Larger straight-winged fighters in USAF inventory couldn't compete with the agility provided by the swept-wing Soviet design. Studies conducted on the airframe of a MiG-15 revealed weak points in its design and aerodynamics. The result was the similarly styled but more advanced F-86 Sabre. *Tyson V. Rininger*

of sound in level flight, it was plagued with stability problems. By the time the D model was introduced, the aircraft had assumed a primary role of ground attack. Practically retired before even making it to the Vietnam War, the McDonnell Douglas F-101 Voodoo was originally overlooked by SAC. However, it caught the eye of the Tactical Air Command (TAC) as a potential high-speed bomber. The aircraft was capable of carrying one nuclear weapon. Eventually the cannons were replaced with cameras and additional radar equipment. It assumed the designation "RF-101C" and took on the aerial reconnaissance role.

The Convair F-102 Delta Dagger was originally designed as a high-speed bomber escort and fighter intercept aircraft. Eventually, the F-102 was equipped with twenty-four 2.75-inch folding fin aerial rockets in the fuselage bay doors that proved highly successful in air-to-ground attacks. The second variation of the F-102, the YF-102B, was so plagued with problems that it eventually became the improved F-106A Delta Dart due to the numerous alterations that essentially created a new aircraft. Unfortunately, the F-106A never saw combat in Vietnam despite the ability to carry up to six AIM-4 Falcon air-to-air missiles. The F-15 became its successor in 1981, and Delta Dart aircraft were passed on to the Air National Guard units.

Like the F-102 and F-106, the Lockheed F-104 Starfighter was intended to be an intercept aircraft. As sleek as the aircraft was and despite the technological advancements it brought to the world of aviation, the USAF saw it as ineffective for the assumed role. The Starfighter simply lacked the payload for a tactical bomber and was unable to match the agility and endurance of other USAF inventory aircraft.

The most successful of the Century Series fighters was the Republic F-105 Thunderchief. Like the F-100 and F-101, the Thunderchief, or "Thud," assumed the role of fighter-bomber with the emphasis on bomber. Capable of carrying a single nuclear weapon as an internal payload along with an external payload larger than that of most World War II bombers, the Thud proved to be a worthy aerial adversary as well. Despite flying the largest single-pilot aircraft ever operated by the USAF, F-105 pilots were able to use the onboard cannons to shoot down nearly thirty enemy aircraft. Nevertheless, the F-105 was not a capable air superiority aircraft. Aircraft still flying after the Vietnam War had just about reached their service life and were deemed obsolete by the USAF.

Originally designed for use by the United States Navy (USN), the McDonnell Douglas F-4C Phantom II was incorporated into the Air Force as its first multi-role specific fighter. Although the F-4 was a potent adversary to the various communist aircraft, the flight characteristics were vastly different. Not only was it big, it was a multi-role aircraft with relatively poor visibility and lacking guns. The roll rate, climb rate, turning capabilities, and other aspects of the more nimble MiGs simply couldn't be duplicated by the Phantom. Despite its perceived deficiencies, the beastly F-4 Phantom did manage 107 MiG kills during the Vietnam War.

The introduction of the Phantom and the desire to concentrate on air superiority created two significant problems for the USAF. The first involved pilot training deficiencies. Instructional pilots flying the adversary role were not specifically trained in the combat tactics of communist air forces and often belonged to the same units as those against whom they were flying. The second problem encompassed the limited maneuvering abilities of a multi-role aircraft.

Noticing these deficiencies, Col. John Boyd developed various aerial maneuverability concepts regarding the new F-4E and its improved flight characteristics. The techniques and proficiency took some time to adopt. The Achilles heel of Boyd's concepts was the aircraft itself along with the constraints of the rules of engagement. Armaments of the F-4E were still limited to the early model AIM-7 and AIM-9 missiles. Because of the conditions of the Vietnam War, visual identification of enemy aircraft was required, resulting in close air combat where missiles were essentially unusable. Adversary aircraft relied heavily on guns, and were quickly taking the upper hand. More experienced pilots did what they could to train others in more successful techniques. Without a proper training exercise, these tactics were taught during combat, resulting in unnecessary losses.

The flow of information regarding the enemy was insufficient. Knowledge of their aircraft characteristics and level of training received were essentially unknown. Because of this, it was difficult to properly train USAF pilots for effective aerial combat. In addition, their aircraft were incapable of properly engaging the enemy with current load standards and flight characteristics. Most importantly, they found themselves being caught by surprise more often than not.

The USAF set forth an immediate study to resolve the problem. Naming it "Red Baron" after the World War I German ace, Manfred von Richthofen, the study showed rotating newer pilots into the combat role was detrimental to their overall success

The evolution of the MiG-15 through MiG-21 shows a growing sleekness to each airframe. From the stubby MiG-15 came the slightly more agile MiG-17 with greater fuel capacity for longer-range missions. The lines of the MiG-17 were tweaked, lengthened, and streamlined to create the MiG-19 with increased velocity and a decreased visual cross section. The MiG-21's remarkable speed and its intercept design made it less agile and removed it from the dogfighting role. *Tyson V. Rininger*

rate. Although this took the USAF by surprise, little could be done to fix the problem. Pilots were needed quickly. More advanced training at that time was simply not possible.

The USAF noticed a new program the USN had developed that incorporated dissimilar aircraft into their training regiment. Realizing it made little sense to dogfight aircraft with similar flight characteristics, the USN implemented Top Gun Fighter Weapons School at Miramar Naval Air Station (NAS), California. Selected pilots were forced to engage against the smaller and more agile McDonnell Douglas A-4 Skyhawk. This enabled the Navy pilots to learn new tactics and push their aircraft to new extremes.

The idea of dissimilar aircraft to create an "aggressor" squadron floated around the USAF for some time. Maj. Gen. R.G. "Zack" Taylor took the opportunity to create the Tactical Fighter Weapons Center by transforming the 4520th Combat Crew Training Wing at Nellis Air Force Base. Taylor saw the great potential of the enormous area surrounding Nellis.

Colonel William L. Kirk at the U.S. Pentagon, also noticed the need for more realistic training exercises. Working as part of the electronic combat directorate, he and members of his Washington, D.C., staff began brainstorming various aspects for improved training. Of note was the Foreign Technology Division at Wright-Patterson Air Force Base in Ohio. The division operated a number of Soviet aircraft that could be utilized to provide a realistic combat environment based on their unique maneuverability and air combat tactics. Unfortunately, the project was soon dismissed due to administration difficulties.

Dissatisfied with the loss rate during the Vietnam War, Air Force Chief of Staff Gen. John D. Ryan

Two F-100D Super Sabre aircraft streak over South Vietnam on their way to an assigned target. The aircraft provided tactical air support to ground forces in Vietnam but was unstable and very difficult to fly. The F100 was the first aircraft in active duty that cruised at supersonic speeds. *USAF*

SAC used the McDonnell F-101 Voodoo as a high-speed bomber. Although the Voodoo was an agile dogfighter under certain circumstances, the aircraft was primarily a bomber. Once engaged by enemy forces, it would often be forced to prematurely drop its payload, thus failing the mission. Chutes deploy on these F-101 Voodoos as they touch down after a training exercise. Both aircraft are from the 107th Fighter Intercept Group, 136th Fighter Intercept Squadron, New York Air National Guard. *USAF*

approved a proposal made by Kirk and Maj. John A. Corder. The proposal was to create an air-to-air aggressor squadron that would utilize surplus Northrop T-38 Talons (as was suggested by Lt. Col. Charles A. Homer). The aggressor squadron would visit other units in the field for training exercises in addition to performing the same task with visiting units at nearby Nellis Range Complex.

In the fall of 1972, the USAF established the 64th Fighter Weapons Squadron. Simulating MiG-21s, the squadron initially flew T-38s. Later, it added F-5E Tiger II aircraft. Exercises utilizing these small, agile aircraft were deemed so successful, the USAF established the 65th Fighter Weapons Squadron as Nellis' second aggressor unit.

With a modified training program finally underway, the USAF was able to accumulate results and statistics on a more favorable path. The Red Baron study led to training pilots on a more personal level. It also provided the avenue for creating an aircraft with a more specific role specializing in air superiority (as compared to the multi-role F-4 Phantom). This desire led to the development of the McDonnell Douglas F-15 Eagle and an entirely new breed of pilots.

DEVELOPMENT OF THE F-15

In the midst of the Vietnam War, the USAF already noticed a trend leading toward losing air supremacy completely. It needed an aircraft devoted to protecting the skies.

Lieutenant Colonel John W. Bohn Jr. devised a plan to replace the multi-role F-4 Phantom with an aircraft specifically designed for aerial combat. This development changed the structure of the USAF by creating a high-low mix of separate air-to-air and air-to-ground combat aircraft. It wanted to develop a high-cost, state-of-the-art aircraft that could defend the skies against Soviet threats while utilizing lower-cost aircraft to handle the ground suppression roles. With the support of Air Force Chief of Staff Gen. John P. McConnell, the study was quickly presented to political members who could put the idea into play.

Primary Function	All-Weather Fighter-Bomber	Type	Number	Remarks
Contractor	McDonnell Aircraft Co., McDonnell Corporation	F-4A	47	USN/USMC; F4H-1F
Powerplant	Two General Electric turbojet engines with afterburners	F-4B	649	USN/USMC; 29 loaned to USAF
		RF-4B	46	USMC; F4H-1P
Thrust	17,900 pounds (8,055 kilograms)	F-4C	583	From F-110A
Length	62 feet 11 inches (19.1 meters)	F-4D	825	Improved F-4C
Height	16 feet 5 inches (5 meters)	F-4E	1,370	Improved F-4D
Wingspan	38 feet 11 inches (11.8 meters)	F-4EJ	140	Japanese F-4E
Speed	Greater than 1,600 mph (Mach 2)	RF-4E	149	Export version
Ceiling	60,000 feet (18,182 meters)	RF-4EJ	14	Japanese RF-4E
Climb Rate	49,000 feet per minute	F-4F	175	Export F-4E for Germany
Max. Takeoff Weight	62,000 pounds (27,900 kilograms)	F-4G	(conv) 116	Wild Weasel
Range	1,300 miles (1,130 nautical miles)	F-4J	522	USN/USMC
Armament	Four AIM-7 Sparrow and four AIM-9M Sidewinder missiles, AGM-65 Maverick missiles, AGM-88 HARM missile capability, one fuselage centerline bomb rack and four pylon bomb racks capable of carrying 12,500 pounds (5,625 kilograms) of general purpose bombs	F-4K	52	Royal Navy; FG.1
		F-4M	118	Royal Air Force; FGR.2
		F-4N	(conv) 228	USN/USMC; from F-4B
		F-4S	(conv) 302	USN/USMC; from F-4J
		F-4T	0	Export proposal
Cost	$18.4 million			
Crew	Two (pilot and electronic warfare officer)			
Date Deployed	May 1963			

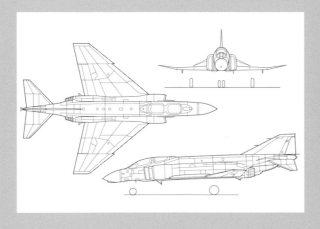

Designed as a multi-role aircraft to replace the Century-Series F-100 through F-106 fighters, the McDonnell Douglas F-4 Phantom incorporated extreme design concepts. Utilizing sharply angled wingtip dihedrals and stabilator anhedrals, the large twin-engine aircraft proved to be a highly maneuverable, multi-service platform for the USAF, USN, and US Marine Corps. Upon development of the Echo model, leading-edge wing slats and an under-the-nose-mounted gun gave the Phantom even greater maneuverability and the ability to engage in close combat dogfighting. Despite the advancements, the aircraft's multi-purpose mission limited its achieving aerial supremacy. *USAF*

Although the Northrop F-5 was suggested as the aircraft most suitable for the air-to-ground role, the Vought A-7 Corsair II assumed that responsibility for both the Air Force and Navy. The large two-seat General Dynamics F-111 Aardvark, with its variable-geometry (VG) swept-wing technology, placed itself out of the range of being a successful air superiority aircraft. It also assumed the role of a more advanced bomber despite the fighter (F) designation. The F-111's failure as a carrier-based fighter for the USN (F-111B), and its inability to fill the USAF preliminary requests for a fighter aircraft, deemed it a political failure. The USN's move to procure the Grumman F-14 Tomcat was a result of lessons learned from the F-111 project. Meanwhile, the USAF still found itself lacking a worthy fighter aircraft.

On June 16, 1965, Headquarters Air Force initiated the Fighter-X (F-X) program with the cooperation of Air Force Systems Command. Within a week, Air Force Systems Command directed the Aeronautical Systems Division to take action on necessary studies for the development of F-X. By December 1965, the official request for "a small, low cost, high performance aircraft capable of visual air-to-ground and air-to-air missions" was submitted with the initial operational capability (IOC) projected for the early 1970s.

This F-104 Starfighter of the 69th Tactical Fighter Training Squadron is part of tactical training at Luke Air Force Base. The missile-like F-104 Starfighter was an engineering marvel. Although it was one of the fastest aircraft in service and capable of very high altitudes, it failed to maintain aerial supremacy against the agile MiG-21 and MiG-23s. *USAF*

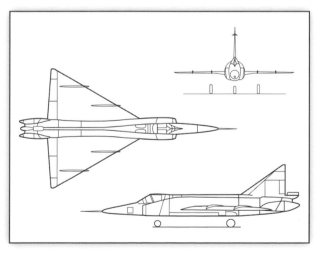

The primary mission of the F-102A was to intercept and destroy enemy aircraft. It completed its maiden flight on October 24, 1953, and was the world's first supersonic, all-weather, jet interceptor and the USAF's first operational, delta-wing aircraft. Although the F-106 replaced it, both aircraft performed poorly when engaged and were only useful in long-range combat. *USAF*

In late 1965, the Secretary of the Air Force, Eugene M. Zuckert, approved $10 million for the 1966 fiscal year toward the study of a new aircraft that could meet the goals set forth by the Aeronautical Systems Division and Air Force Systems Command. Proposals for a tactical support aircraft were devised according to the Aerospace Contractor Studies (ACS). In January 1966, the proposals were distributed to thirteen different companies. Within several months, eight companies responded.

By August, Headquarters Air Force selected three manufacturers to participate in a four-month concept

Ground crewmen remove wing tanks from F-106 Delta Dart aircraft. These aircraft are at the base to compete in the William Tell Weapons Meet 1984 and are from the 102nd Fighter Interceptor Wing, Massachusetts Air National Guard. The F-106s of the 87th Fighter Interceptor Squadron sit at the end of the row. The F-106 became an incredible intercept aircraft during the 1970s and 1980s though maneuverability had been sacrificed for speed. *USAF*

formulation study. Lockheed Martin, North American, and Boeing submitted a combined 500 designs by October 1967. All of them were rejected.

Reflective of the Tactical Fighter Experimental (TFX) program requested of manufacturers a few years earlier, VG swept-wing technology took the forefront in design submissions. Concepts learned from the F-111 program, along with a strong desire to capitalize on a multi-role airframe, failed to meet USAF requests for an advanced air-to-air fighter.

Concerns about bringing a fighter to fruition escalated in 1967 when the Soviets introduced the MiG-25 Foxbat at the Domodedovo Air Show. The aircraft, designed to intercept the Lockheed A-12/SR-71 and North American XB-70 Valkyrie, could achieve speeds of Mach 2.8. No fighter in the U.S.

arsenal was capable of engaging the MiG-25. The only potential aircraft, the A-12 operated by the U.S. Central Intelligence Agency, was deemed impractical. Eventually, it was learned that the MiG-25 was not as capable as first thought. It was, however, enough to speed up production of a new fighter. A second draft called for another Request for Proposals (RFP) based on an airframe that could specifically combat the MiG-25.

Issued on August 11, 1967, the second RFP unveiled the name of the program that would eventually lead to the F-15. Commonly referred to as "Fighter-Experimental," the F-X program was intended to be read as "Fighter-Unknown."

Earlier studies, conducted by then Major Boyd, came to light that regarded a mathematical formula used to determine the most efficient use of an aircraft's kinetic energy and maneuverability. The study, published in May 1964, was named the "Energy Maneuverability Theory." It didn't receive much attention until this time. The theory allowed designers the ability to work from charts and graphs to design an efficient airframe capable of the agility requested by the RFP as well as what would be within the realms of pilot G-tolerance.

During this time, the National Aeronautics and Space Administration's (NASA) Langley Research Center was reviewing submissions by McDonnell Douglas, North American, and Fairchild-Republic. Since the Langley Research Center had developed much of the technology that would be incorporated into a next-generation fighter, they requested to be a part of the submission proposal process.

Dr. John Foster, Director of the Defense Department Research and Engineering, was pivotal to the design process. He headed the RFP fulfillment to the Department of Defense (DoD). Foster based his involvement on two forms of reasoning: Development of the F-15 would require such advanced concepts and materials that civilian contractors may run into limitations on available resources. Second, NASA felt that its problem-solving expertise would limit risks to the project and safety to those involved.

NASA narrowed down the design proposals to four concepts: LFAX-4, 8, 9, and 10. The first two concepts, LFAX-4 and LFAX-8, utilized the same fuselage with varying wing configurations. A swept wing was incorporated in LFAX-4 that later played a large role in the development of the Grumman F-14 Tomcat while LFAX-8 instituted a fixed-sweep variant. A wing-mounted twin-engine variant was the result of LFAX-9, and visual studies of the MiG-25 Foxbat showed up heavily in the design elements of the LFAX-10.

Working closely with NASA and heeding the results of wind-tunnel tests, as well as lessons learned regarding the advantages and disadvantages of the VG wing configuration, McDonnell Douglas chose to perfect the fixed swept-wing design. This saved an enormous amount of weight by doing without the swing-wing mechanism and pivot structure. Concepts utilizing the VG configuration were chosen

Here an F-105D is fully laden with dumb bombs and prepared for a ground-assault mission. The F-105 Thunderchief, or Thud, was arguably one of the most successful aircraft of the Century Series fighters. It was used primarily as a bomber with minimal, one-on-one capability. *USAF*

The F-105 was the largest single-pilot aircraft used by the USAF. A two-seat F-105F is shown here with a full complement of arms. Although the F-105 performed well, the airframe was obsolete by the end of the Vietnam War. The F-4 Phantom fit the role of fighter for a short time, but it was typically used as a bomber. *USAF*

by Lockheed, General Dynamics, and Grumman. Such concepts combined with large engines and an aircrew of two, resulted in airframe designs up to 60,000 pounds.

The McDonnell Douglas, or "McAir" as the USAF commonly referred to them, had a fixed wing, single-pilot design that brought the weight down to a manageable 40,000 pounds. Designs by the VG advocates were reaching weights of up to 60,000 pounds with a thrust-to-weight ratio capable of intercepting the Foxbat becoming insurmountable.

It was determined that the F-X would be a single-seat aircraft. This reduced the increasing weight projections being submitted. Eliminating the redundant backseat gear, a savings of approximately 5,000 pounds, was mostly the doing of combat veteran Col. John J. Burns. His experience in single-seat aircraft during World War II and Korea proved a solo pilot could handle the workload of the newly devised weapons safety officer (WSO) position as found on the F-4. Furthermore, two-crew communication efforts simply added to the confusion during tense combat situations. Ground-based radar stations were sufficient to warn a solo pilot of potential problems. The USAF agreed with Colonel Burns' ideas for an advanced radar system that could be operated by a single pilot.

While airframe design encompassed the majority of manufacturers, other aspects of the F-X, such as avionics and powerplant, needed to be developed in synchronization. According to the latest RFP, avionics were to include an advanced radar system capable of detecting aircraft like the Foxbat at long range. Originally an acronym for Radio Detection and Ranging, radar had only a forward-looking ability in aircraft of the day.

The Foxbat wasn't the only fighter the F-X would be up against. Lessons learned in the Korean and Vietnam Wars called for a radar that could find small radar-cross-section targets like the MiG-21 as well as decipher from the ground clutter at lower altitudes. The pulse-Doppler system would work best. Both Hughes and Westinghouse managed to devise a Doppler system capable of fitting within the airframe of the F-X profile.

The Doppler radar measures the radial velocity of targets in the antenna's directional beam. Essentially, the radar shifts the received frequency up or down based on the radial velocity of the target by concentrating or relaxing the beam. Although the Doppler system wasn't perfect, add-on computer systems were able to filter false ground-returns by eliminating anything relative to the speed of the operating aircraft. Finding aircraft at a ninety-degree angle remained a problem. Radar saw the aircraft as travelling at the same speed relative to the earth so the filter cancelled out the return.

In March 1968, Hughes and Westinghouse competed for the contract by developing a long-range, look-down radar. Hughes developed a pulse-Doppler radar capable of detecting ground targets as well as aerial targets in all-weather conditions. The radar unit also had add-on versatility for optical tracking

systems as technology might allow in later years. The USAF awarded an $82 million contract to Hughes on September 30, 1970, to develop what would later become the AN/APG-63 radar.

Of course, this project wasn't going anywhere without the proper engines. At the time, jet propulsion had only been around for twenty years. The high-bypass turbofan had become the most popular engine to date. The idea was to combine high-bypass technology with an afterburning stage enabling the aircraft to have a boost of acceleration when needed.

Colonel Boyd, a test pilot and Korean War veteran, was a highly influential combat strategist who had a theory about what engine would work best in a combat situation. The Air Force Strategic Command's (AFSC) wanted a versatile engine to aim for a bypass ratio of approximately 2.2:1 (2.2 volumes of air through the fan bypass for each equivalent

The F-4 Phantom was a pivotal fighter in the development of multi-role capabilities. With the design of faster jet aircraft and beyond-visual-range technology, the F-4E and the inclusion of a powerful gun put USAF air supremacy back on track. *Tyson V. Rininger*

volume of air through the core section of the turbojet, or "afterburner"). Boyd's idea was to reduce that number to a nearly even 1:1 ratio for more efficient afterburner operations during combat maneuvering. Having done combat tactic studies of the MiG versus the F-86, he figured pilots would rather have a more efficient afterburner despite the slightly greater fuel consumption.

General Electric (GE) and Pratt & Whitney (P&W) were both given the challenge to meet the AFSC's goal of a 1.5:1 bypass ratio, meeting Boyd's suggestion halfway. In the meantime, AFSC's Aeronautical Propulsion Laboratory was tasked with doing an independent evaluation.

Despite the disappointments of the F-111 and F-14A's P&W TF30 powerplant, Dr. Harold Brown required the USN and USAF to work together in developing a common core for use in the F-X program as well as a replacement engine for the F-14A. Coincidentally, Brown, DoD Director of Defense Research and Engineering, was the author of the failed TFX program. While GE and P&W were working on the engine development, it was Brown's study of the existing platforms that determined a bypass ratio of 0.6:1 was most beneficial.

By September 1967, GE and P&W had completed their studies, and the USAF authorized the joint development program. Dubbed the "advanced turbine engine gas generator" (ATEGG), contractors took advantage of the faults learned from the TF-30 program. They worked to reduce overall weight and increase thrust. A final RFP was sent to GE and P&W as well as General Motors (GM) in April 1968.

The U.S. Air Force established the 64th Fighter Weapons Squadron to improve aerial combat tactics. The nimble F-5E Tiger II (inset) had the responsibility of simulating the agile MiG-21 (pictured above). F-5Es routinely flew simulated combat sorties against F-4E pilots at Nellis Air Force Base. The USAF hoped to gain the upper hand against the Soviet-supplied MiGs with their improved tactics. *Tyson V. Rininger*

The common compressor-turbine core was proclaimed as the winning concept on February 27, 1970. The design of the ATEGG was furthered by P&W with an awarded $448 million contract utilizing technologies already tapped upon in existing engines. Slightly modified components from the Lockheed SR-71 Blackbird's J58 engine were combined with the TF30-P-1 from the F-111, and the TF30-P-412 from the F-14, to construct a standard core for use by the USN and USAF.

Although the idea of building a common core seemed like a good one, differences in USAF and USN aircraft requirements were far too great for the program to succeed. The USN was running short on funds and already had a working engine, albeit problematic. Funds destined for a replacement to the TF30-P-412 were diverted

to purchase more F-14s. Though the decision of the USN to back out of the development program didn't come overnight, it did eventually cost the USAF $110 million to revert to a single service contract.

In the meantime, various aircraft manufacturers were still contending for the F-X airframe design. A division between the VG airframes and the fixed-wing designs seemed to be the dominating factor in how the USAF approached the vastly different concepts. On December 1, 1967, the USAF selected one manufacturer from each of the two configurations: General Dynamics, with their experience in the development of the variable-geometry swept-wing F-111, and McDonnell Douglas, with their fixed swept-wing design. They were to create a second concept formulation study.

The MiG-25 Foxbat had enormous exhaust nozzles with incredible power thrust. It was capable of nearly Mach 3, threatened high-altitude surveillance aircraft like the SR-71 and could intercept everything in the U.S. inventory. American aircraft manufacturers scrambled to create a new fighter to combat this threat. *USAF, Soviet Military Power*

COLONEL JOHN BOYD

Dubbed "Forty-Second Boyd," Colonel John Boyd wagered any pilot that, despite a position of disadvantage, he could engage in forty seconds or less. While working with the Fighter Weapons School at Nellis Air Force Base, from 1954 to 1960, he never lost a bet.

Boyd enlisted with the U.S. Army Air Corps and served from 1945 to 1947. From 1951 to 1975, he served as an officer with the U.S. Air Force. Despite Boyd's incredible flying skills and theories that put tactical air-superiority concepts on its head, early cancellation of a tour in Vietnam left him with no air-to-air victories.

Boyd is best known for his strategies. He realized that current U.S. Air Force training programs were far from adequate and devised procedures that fully trained pilots into fighter pilots before putting them in combat situations. Boyd also understood that pilots learned less training against similar airframes and proposed training against more agile, dissimilar aircraft. These two points eventually led to the Fighter Weapons School at Nellis Air Force Base, Nevada. This training evolved into one of the most intense training exercises in the world, Red Flag.

Boyd had always been comfortable with mathematics. He constantly utilized quantum mechanics, advanced calculus, aerodynamic principles, the physics of subatomic particles, and other math principles. His mathematical interests eventually led him to biological studies that furthered his breadth of theories. Two of his most well-known ideas stretched the limits of both mathematical and biological concepts.

Working with civilian mathematician Thomas Christie, Boyd developed the groundbreaking, Energy-Maneuverability (E-M) theory of aerial combat. This theory practically saved the F-X program. It assisted developers in obtaining a logical design based on wing efficiency and applicable maneuvering tactics. It was, in part, due to the E-M theory that both the General Dynamics F-16 "Fighting Falcon" and the Boeing F/A-18 "Hornet" came into existence. Boyd proved that a small aircraft could be just as successful in combat situations as a larger, more powerful airframe. Even though the USAF objected to the production of the F-16, the airframe was eventually produced in the thousands and sold to more than twenty countries. It is the only fighter produced that cost less than its predecessor.

One of Boyd's most accepted ideas was the OODA Loop, originally called the "Boyd Cycle." It applied to the decision-making cycle of a business or entity. Although originally devised as a means of making a decision more quickly than an opponent during air-to-air combat, it was soon adopted and applied to mainstream business practice.

Boyd noted that all intelligent life interacts with its environment in a looping series of processes resulting in the famed acronym OODA:

- Observation: the collection of data by means of the senses
- Orientation: the analysis and synthesis of data to form one's current mental perspective
- Decision: the determination of a course of action based on one's current mental perspective
- Action: the physical playing-out of decisions

Boyd was not without controversy. His combative and often confrontational style of discussion led to another nickname, "Genghis John." Despite his legendary concepts, incredible flying skills, and devotion to the advancement of air supremacy techniques, Boyd had just as many enemies as allies. He routinely went against the grain of authority to do what he believed in. The biggest result of his tenacity was the USAF procurement of the F-16.

Following his retirement from the USAF in 1970, Boyd went to work as a consultant in the tactical air office for the Office of the Assistant Secretary of Defense for Program Analysis and Evaluation. Boyd was pivotal in the success of the first Gulf War's invasion of Iraq. Later, Boyd was credited with devising the "left hook" plan of attack for invading Iraq during Operation Desert Storm.

Boyd reportedly requested no pay for his time while working in the Pentagon. He told a friend, "Two ways to be free: to become rich, or to cut your needs to the bone." Never thinking he'd be a wealthy man, he opted for the latter. His disciplined lifestyle gained him the recognition of yet another nickname, "Ghetto Colonel."

Boyd was the recipient of numerous accommodation medals, including four-time honoree of the Legion of Merit. Over the years, he was also awarded the Air Force Association Citation of Honor, USAF Systems Command Scientific Achievement Award, USAF Research and Development Award, and the Dr. Harold Brown Award for his work on the Energy-Maneuverability concept.

Boyd was given full military honors at Arlington National Cemetery after passing away at the age of seventy on March 9, 1997.

Even though the overall design was being narrowed, the USAF still faced internal disagreements about F-X's exact role. Strategic Air Command insisted on an air-to-air fighter while the Secretary of the Air Force saw potential in the multi-role platform.

Both sides still had to face HQ TAC (which had gone through multiple changes during the course of the project).

Tactical Air Command had evolved into a combat command responsible for supplying units and trained

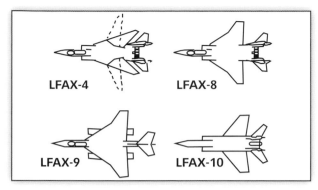

NASA narrowed aircraft design proposals to four concepts, LFAX-4, 8, 9, and 10. Two of these, LFAX-4 and LFAX-8, utilized the same fuselage with varying wing configurations. The LFAX-4 used a sweep-wing. The LFAX-8 instituted a fixed-sweep variant. The LFAX-9 had a wing-mounted, twin-engine variant. Visual studies of the MiG-25 Foxbat showed up heavily in the design elements of the LFAX-10. Ultimately, the F-15 incorporated many aspects of the LFAX-8. *NASA*

aircrews to the United States Air Forces Europe (USAFE) and the Pacific Air Command (PACAF). The combined forces unit, known as "Tactical Air Forces" (TAF), had learned of the inadequacies of the multi-role F-4 in combat over the Southeast Asian skies. In February 1968, TAC issued the required operational capability statement noting that only an air superiority fighter would be accepted as a replacement for the F-4 Phantom II.

As the F-X project came closer to reality and concepts were narrowed down, interdepartmental disagreements became more vocal and specific. While both TAF and the USAF chief of staff were in agreement regarding the concept of an air superiority fighter, the civilian sector of the USAF was determined that it be a multi-role aircraft. Two items that TAF wanted to eliminate were the

Carrying four AA-6 Acrid missiles, the Soviet MiG-25 Foxbat threatened American aerial supremacy. In response, intelligent twin-fin, multi-engine, swept delta-wing concepts made their way on to the F-15. Although concerns later waned, fears were addressed with the development of the more advanced F-15. *USAF, Soviet Military Power*

all-weather bombing system and the accompanying ground terrain radar system.

To further the problem, Boyd and other pilots, who had experience flying against the MiG-15 through 21 series of aircraft in Southeast Asia and North Vietnam, were anything but optimistic. They couldn't grasp how a 40,000-pound aircraft could be an effective dogfighter. They saw the program as a new generation F-4. They became known as the "Fighter Mafia" and eventually played a large role in the development of the lighter, single-engine F-16.

As requirements were narrowed and potential advancements in technology realized, the most concise RFP was issued in September 1968 to the original seven companies. This third RFP for the F-X project called for a single-seat, Mach 2.5-capable, high thrust-to-weight ratio airframe with 360-degree cockpit visibility. Flight characteristics needed to include a wing design with a high load factor and buffet-free performance up to Mach 0.9, along with a global ferry range. Additional factors included a long-range pulse-Doppler radar and advanced cockpit design with heads-up display (HUD) capability. Structural factors would include a

The XB-70 Valkyrie was under development when word of the MiG-25 Foxbat raised attention at the Pentagon. The Foxbat was designed to intercept and attack high-speed, high-altitude bombers such as the XB-70 and the seemingly impervious SR-71 Blackbird. The downward angled wing tips of this XB-70 indicate that it is in cruise mode. *USAF*

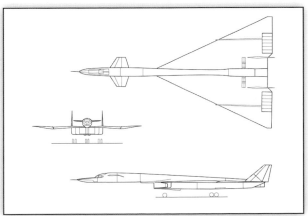

ABOVE The North American F-86 Sabre was an update to the FJ Fury series of aircraft. The U.S. Navy needed a swept-wing, carrier-based fighter and to overcome weaknesses found on the MiG-15. The result was the potent F-86. The Sabre became critical to restoring air supremacy over Southeast Asia in both the Korean and Vietnam Wars. *Tyson V. Rininger*

LEFT The XB-70A Valkyrie was one of the world's most exotic bombers. The Valkyrie was a high-altitude bomber that could fly three times the speed of sound. It made its initial flight on September 21, 1964. *NASA*

Problems with the P&W TF30-P-412 installed in the F-14A Tomcat led the USAF to devise a joint program with the USN to develop the F100-PW-100. Because of massive modifications required for USN aircraft and escalating costs, the USN dropped out of the program. *Tyson V. Rininger*

high-time aircraft fatigue factor of no less than 4,000 hours leading to an improved structure design able to protect hydraulic and fight control systems, as well as the electric and fuel system, in a combat environment. Finally, the aircraft had to be self-sufficient without the need for ground support equipment.

Having thrown out the VG concept altogether, the USAF awarded McDonnell Douglas, Fairchild Hiller, and North American Rockwell each a $15.4 million contract to provide a final design by June 30, 1969. All three manufacturers managed to submit their proposals on time to the USAF's F-15 Systems Project Office. Officially established in June 1967 by the Aeronautical Systems Division, the F-X Systems Project Office spent the next six months scouring over the research data and design concepts. McDonnell Douglas alone submitted 37,000 pages of data supporting their design.

Although McDonnell Douglas spent a majority of their time and effort on the USN's VFX project, James S. "Sandy" McDonnell wisely appointed some six hundred employees, many of whom were McAir's top engineers, to work on the F-X program. To intensify the importance of winning the F-X contract, McAir moved the F-X assigned staff into Building One at their St. Louis based facility. Their experience with the VFX program and understanding the USAF's desires were cruicial to the final design submission.

On December 23, 1969, USAF systems program manager for the newly named F-15, Brig. Gen. Benjamin N. Bellis, personally awarded McDonnell Douglas the F-X contract. Together with Hughes Aircraft Company and Pratt & Whitney, the F-15 was on its way to becoming the most technologically advanced, powerful, and maneuverable aircraft ever to take to the skies.

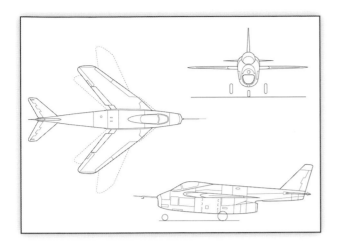

The first swing-wing aircraft, an X-5 (50-1838), arrived at Edwards Air Force Base on June 9, 1951. Bell Company test pilot Jean "Skip" Ziegler made the initial Phase I flights eleven days later. Major Frank Everest flew six flights during December 1951 and January 1952. After a final flight by Everest on January 8, 1952, the first X-5 was turned over to the NACA. The second X-5 (50-1839) had also been delivered by this time. Variable swept wings were a design feature in aircraft from the 1960s into the 1980s. These included the F-111, F-14, and B-1 in the United States; the Su-22 and Su-24 attack aircraft and the Tu-22M and Tu-160 strategic bombers built in the Soviet Union; and the European Tornado strike aircraft and interceptor. *NASA*

The U.S. Navy eventually considered the F-111 Aardvark useless and the TFX program a failure. Although swing-wing technology was still sought after and included as one of the four LFAX concepts, variable-wing geometry was dropped in favor of a fixed-swept design. Ultimately, variable-wing geometry did find its way onto a successful fighter in the form of the F-14 Tomcat. *Tyson V. Rininger*

MCDONNELL DOUGLAS AIRCRAFT COMPANY

The joint efforts of two aeronautical pioneers resulted in the largest defense contractor in the United States. Through a storied history, the efforts of Donald Douglas and James Smith McDonnell created the largest developer of military aircraft, third-largest NASA contractor, and the world's third-largest supplier of commercial aircraft behind Boeing and French manufacturer Airbus.

Fascinated with flight since witnessing the Wright Brothers exhibition for the U.S. Army in 1908, Douglas entered the Naval Academy for two years and finished his mechanical engineering degree at the Massachusetts Institute of Technology. Following his graduation in 1915, aircraft designer Glenn Martin, of Martin Marietta fame, offered him a position. With the start of war in Europe, Douglas relocated to Washington D.C., where he assisted the Signal Corps for only a few months before returning to Martin's company out of frustration.

Douglas continued working with Martin until 1920 when he established his own business in Los Angeles. With help from a financial backer, Douglas designed his first aircraft, the "Cloudster," capable of cross-country flight because it reached altitudes higher than the previously restrictive mountain ranges. In 1921, he established the Douglas Company and was asked to produce a torpedo plane, dubbed the DT, for use by the U.S. Navy. Following the DT's success, he went on to produce the World Cruiser in 1924, a plane that circumnavigated the globe in fifteen days and put the small Douglas Company on the map.

Douglas's first major challenge came in response to a letter by Jack Frye of Trans-World Airlines (TWA) regarding a challenge to better a design submitted by William Boeing's United Company. Boeing promised a tri-motor aircraft capable of flying twelve passengers at 145 miles per hour. Douglas met the challenge by devising an aircraft that could carry fourteen passengers at a speed of almost 180 miles per hour using only two engines. The aircraft, designated DC-1, went through so many changes before delivery that it was redesignated DC-2. The DC-2 (Douglas Commercial) production granted so many insights into commercial aircraft design that the venerable DC-3 became the first mainstream aircraft capable of providing revenue by flying only passengers.

The DC-3 proved so popular that the aircraft dominated almost eighty percent of commercial airline service. At the outbreak of World War II, Douglas prepared the DC-3 for multi-role purposes as both a commercial and military platform. Modified for use both as a personnel carrier, C-47, and as a bomber, B-18, the DC-3 was also used as an airborne gunship, AC-47, providing close-in air support. The Army Air Corps eventually constructed more than 10,000 DC-3 airframes.

Following World War II, Douglas's newest competitor, Lockheed, provided TWA with the revolutionary Constellation aircraft designed by Howard Hughes. A response to the "Connie" resulted in the DC-6. The following DC-7 became the first commercial transport capable of flying nonstop coast-to-coast, regardless of headwinds. The DC series of aircraft were chosen as the first presidential transports, such as the DC-4/C-54, dubbed by Roosevelt as the "Sacred Cow," and Truman's DC-6 /C-118, named "Independence."

Douglas's hesitancy to compete in the jet age led to the company's downward turn. While Boeing's chief test pilot, "Tex" Hill, was completing barrel rolls over Seattle in the new four-engined, jet-powered 707, Douglas's competing DC-8 was still undergoing wind tunnel testing. Douglas's most loyal customer, American Airlines, was enticed by Boeing's 707. This forced Douglas to accelerate the DC-8 program. As a result, United Airlines, typically associated with Boeing, became the first buyer of the DC-8.

Unfortunately, haste in development and increased competition posed by Boeing resulted in Douglas's inability to provide aircraft as quickly as promised. As backorders rose, the company began losing clients to Boeing. In an effort to maintain an industry presence, Douglas introduced the DC-9 that, like the similarities of the DC-8 compared to the 707, closely resembled the new Boeing 727. Instead of wing-mounted engines, both the DC-9 and 727 incorporated rear fuselage-mounted engines. In 1966, despite the limited success of the DC-8 and DC-9, Douglas was still losing money and financiers reduced their backing.

Founding J.S. McDonnell & Associates in 1928, McDonnell was a graduate of Princeton University with a Master of Science in Aeronautical Engineering from MIT. Like Douglas, McDonnell also went to work for the Martin Company but did so as a result of closing his business due to the Great Depression. After resigning from Martin in 1938, he founded the McDonnell Aircraft Corporation in St. Louis, Missouri, and intended to create aircraft for the general consumer. He quickly became one of the largest suppliers of U.S. military aircraft.

McDonnell had a deep interest in the occult and the paranormal and as a result, spooky names were given to many of his aircraft designs, such as the XF-85 Goblin, F2H Banshee, F3H Demon, F-101 Voodoo, F-4 Phantom, and even the Gargoyle guided missile. Another example of his fascination with the paranormal was the founding of the McDonnell Laboratory for Psychical Research that provided facilities for scientists to study parapsychology, extrasensory perception, mind control, and the ability to predict the future.

Although McDonnell remained small in comparison to Douglas, employing slightly over 5,000 people compared to Douglas's 160,000, both companies were forced to make huge cutbacks in work staff following World War II. While Douglas took on Boeing and Lockheed for shares of the commercial aviation market, McDonnell enlisted the help of Dave Lewis, making him the company's Chief of Aerodynamics. The McDonnell Aircraft Corporation became a family affair with the inclusion of his two sons, James III and John, along with his nephew Sanford. In 1958, Lewis became Executive Vice President, followed by Chief Operating Officer in 1962.

With the Korean and Vietnam Wars, McDonnell found itself a major supplier of aircraft to the U.S. Navy and U.S. Air Force with types like the F2H Banshee, F3H Demon, F-101 Voodoo, and Lewis's highly successful multi-role F-4 Phantom II. Douglas continued to do their part with the A-4 Skyhawk and F4D Skyray, but it still was not enough due to overexerting themselves with the DC-8 and DC-9.

Experienced in producing missiles, both companies were eager to take part in the new rocket era brought about by NASA. While Douglas worked on the Zeus, Delta, and Saturn projects, McDonnell constructed the Mercury and Gemini capsules.

By 1963, Douglas was still in financial difficulty and on the defensive. Takeover bids were offered by six different companies: North American Aviation, Martin Marietta, General Dynamics, Fairchild, McDonnell, and Signal Oil & Gas. With Lewis having been made president of McDonnell and the company's history of effective management, Douglas chose to sell to McDonnell on April 28, 1967. Prior to the acquisition of Douglas, McDonnell divided their company into three separate divisions. Adding Douglas simply created a fourth division. This eased the merger process and created the McDonnell Douglas Company (MDC).

Following the merger, Donald Douglas Jr. was gradually excluded from the board of directors and eventually left the company. Sanford McDonnell was made Chief Executive Officer after James McDonnell's retirement in 1971.

Projects currently underway, like the A-4 Skyhawk and F-4 Phantom II, were continued under the new unification. The first new project tackled by MDC was the wide body DC-10 intended to compete with Boeing's enormous 747. Capable of carrying more than 450 passengers with fewer engines than the Boeing alternative, the DC-10 seemed like a formidable competitor. Unfortunately Boeing had already beat MCD to the market and after a few modifications, the 747 proved to be a quite capable platform. With the late introduction of the DC-10, few potential customers remained and sales were sparse.

Concentrating once more on the military market, McDonnell Douglas played a large role in the creation of the AV-8 Harrier licensed by Hawker Siddeley. The company went on to manufacture the F-15 Eagle and F/A-18 Hornet. In 1984, MCD acquired Hughes Helicopters from the Summa Corporation, resulting in the McDonnell Douglas Helicopter Company. The most successful project to result from the acquisition was the AH-64 Apache.

Creation of the MD-11 was a response to the increasing black eye posed by the DC-10. On May 25, 1979, a DC-10 suffered engine failure on take off and lost all 273 people on board. Although blame fell to American Airlines for poor maintenance, the public viewed the airframe as the problem. The answer was a redesign of the aircraft, renamed MD-11, which enabled it to carry 405 passengers over a range of almost 9,000 miles with a flight crew of two.

While Boeing and Airbus were devising new aircraft for the market, MCD chose a slightly different route and introduced a new aircraft without building one. A major update to the DC-9 was marketed as the MD-80, named for the year of its design. At half the cost of a comparable Boeing 757, MCD offered to lend the aircraft to American Airlines for a five-year term instead of the usual eighteen-year lease.

As the Cold War came to an end and military subsidies dried up in the early 1990s, McDonnell Douglas no longer had a reliable income. The MD-11 and MD-80 proved less popular than hoped and drew further monetary resources from the company. In 1988, the founder's son, John F. McDonnell, was selected to be the chief executive officer and tasked with solving the company's $3.3 billion debt. In doing so, McDonnell cut the work force by forty percent and reduced the company's annual operating costs by $700 million. Unable to rely on military contracts, McDonnell chose to make the commercial airline business its main area of growth.

Going head-to-head with Boeing, MCD released the MD-12 concept, a wide-body, double-deck jumbo jet. With Boeing controlling fifty-five percent of the commercial airline market and offering five different airframe models at the time, McDonnell Douglas sought the help of outside partners.

Although the MD-12 never made it to fruition, MCD's new business strategy, set forth in the late 1980s, placed them in a more suitable position than other aviation manufacturers who had suffered the same economic downfall. With fewer competitors and increased mergers and acquisitions, McDonnell Douglas secured more military contracts and by 1992, showed an earnings increase of 145 percent from the previous year.

Despite their revival and the continued success of the F-15 Eagle, including foreign sales, McDonnell Douglas received intense pressure from Boeing. In 1997, Boeing merged with MCD in a $13 billion stock-swap resulting in the Boeing Company. Boeing took over the production and maintenance of the F-15 Eagle and F-15E Strike Eagle as well as the development of the F/A-18 variants.

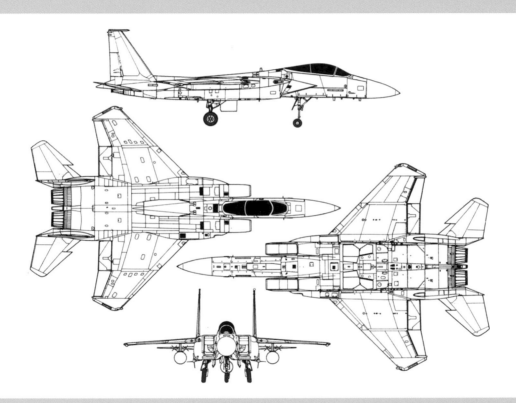

This illustration shows the layout and panel structure of the F-15A Eagle. The few changes from design to construction were a much larger airbrake and removal of the high-maintenance exhaust "Turkey Feather" plates. The illustration also displays the Conformal Fuel Tanks (CFT) in the head-on graphic. Few changes were made between the A and C models of the Eagle. *Richard Ferriere*

CHAPTER TWO

F-15 DEVELOPMENT

EFFECTIVE FEBRUARY 27, 1970, CONTRACT F33657-70-C-0300 with McDonnell Douglas signaled the go-ahead for full development of the F-15. That same day, P&W received a $448 million contract for development of the F100-PW-100 engines. As development progressed, Hughes was selected on April 8, 1971, as the subcontractor to produce the AN/APG-63 radar system. Exactly two months later, the critical design review of the F-15 was complete.

Here is how the DoD defines critical design review:

A technical review that may be conducted to determine that the detailed design satisfies the performance and engineering requirements of the development specification; to establish the detailed design compatibility among the item and other items of equipment, facilities, computer programs and algorithms, and personnel; to assess producibility and risk areas; and to review the preliminary product baseline specifications. Normally conducted during the System Development and Demonstration (SDD) phase.

Contract details called for twenty initial airframes for testing purposes separated into three phases. The first twelve test aircraft for Phase I were assigned to the Contractor Development Test and Evaluation unit. It consisted of aircraft builds 71-0280–71-0291. Eight

With Day-Glo orange highlights, F-1 Eagle 71-0280 flies over Edwards Air Force Base in the Central California desert. Tasked with testing airframe and wing design flight characteristics, this Eagle first took to the skies on July 27, 1972. The pilot, Irving L. Burrows, penetrated the speed of sound within a week of its initial flight. A total of twelve aircraft tested various components, including avionics, weapons systems, powerplant, and handling characteristics. *USAF*

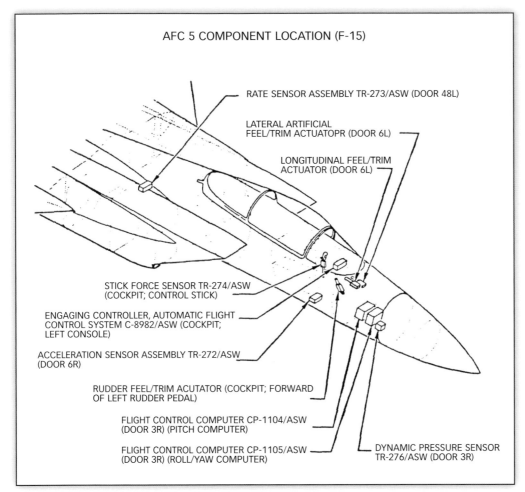

AFC 5 COMPONENT LOCATION (F-15)

RATE SENSOR ASSEMBLY TR-273/ASW (DOOR 48L)

LATERAL ARTIFICIAL FEEL/TRIM ACTUATOPR (DOOR 6L)

LONGITUDINAL FEEL/TRIM ACTUATOR (DOOR 6L)

STICK FORCE SENSOR TR-274/ASW (COCKPIT; CONTROL STICK)

ENGAGING CONTROLLER, AUTOMATIC FLIGHT CONTROL SYSTEM C-8982/ASW (COCKPIT; LEFT CONSOLE)

ACCELERATION SENSOR ASSEMBLY TR-272/ASW (DOOR 6R)

RUDDER FEEL/TRIM ACUTATOR (COCKPIT; FORWARD OF LEFT RUDDER PEDAL)

FLIGHT CONTROL COMPUTER CP-1104/ASW (DOOR 3R) (PITCH COMPUTER)

FLIGHT CONTROL COMPUTER CP-1105/ASW (DOOR 3R) (ROLL/YAW COMPUTER)

DYNAMIC PRESSURE SENSOR TR-276/ASW (DOOR 3R)

The F-15's state-of-the-art, automated flight control system assisted the pilot with more efficient handling of the aircraft and reduced fatigue. Designed as a dual-channel, three-axis system, the control augmentation system (CAS) received electronic signals from rudder and stick inputs and filtered out unwanted movements such as those caused by turbulence. These components allowed for a much smoother flight. *USAF*

Eagles, numbers 72-0113–72-0120, were assigned to the Phase II program, Air Force Development Test and Evaluation.

Aircraft from both Phase I and II were sent to Edwards Air Force Base where test pilots from McDonnell Douglas and the USAF awaited as part of the F-15 Joint Test Force, as well as maintenance and support personnel who had been working on the project since its initial feasibility stage. The Joint Test Force consisted of eleven pilots from McDonnell Douglas and ten from Air Force System Command's 6512th Test Squadron, 6510 Test Wing.

Phase III aircraft were not of the initial twenty, but consisted of airframes 73-0085–73-0114, and participated in Follow-on Operational Test and Evaluation. Seven aircraft were flown by pilots from TAC's 422nd Fighter Weapons Squadron based at Luke Air Force Base as part of the 57th Fighter Weapons Wing.

Prior to arriving at Edwards, models of various shapes and sizes underwent testing in all types of conditions. More than one hundred configurations combining different fuselage shapes with different wing designs amassed over 23,000 hours of wind tunnel testing. The final design became known to the McDonnell Douglas team as the "199-B." The 199-B utilized a cambered wing with a forty-five-degree swept leading edge. Unlike its predecessor, the F-4 Phantom, the 199-B did not make use of slats or anhedral/dihedral wing surfaces.

The first F-15 constructed (71-0280), dubbed "F-1," put the wing and fuselage design to the test as part of the Phase I team. Its construction was proof of the advancements McDonnell Douglas incorporated into the construction process. Build-time and

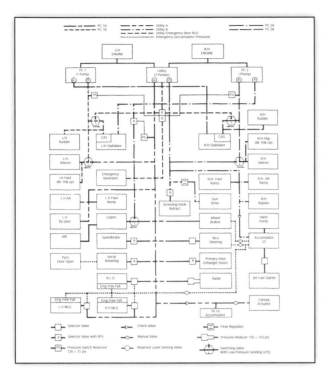

The F-15's hydro-mechanical system included a redundant system in the case of structural or mechanical failure. It was further aided by a series of rods and pulleys attached to hydraulic actuators for ease of input. The system incorporated a pitch and roll aid to compensate for adverse yaw and roll at supersonic speeds. This schematic illustrates the complex, interconnected system that enabled pilots to fly confidently in changing flight characteristics over the course of a single mission. *USAF*

structural life were increased in the manufacturing process by combining only three main elements to form the aircraft compared to the myriad of components needed to assemble the F-4. Fuselage simplicity cut down on the number of man-hours needed for assembly and increased the fatigue-life of the Eagle's structure to 4,000 hours, three times that of the F-4.

As construction continued, weight savings became prevalent. Hand-braided wire bundling, extensive use of aluminum and titanium, as well as honeycomb designs, helped to shave 6,000 pounds off the airframe, compared to the similarly sized Phantom. Engineers chose to use billet titanium components weighing only 145 pounds for the rigid bulkheads. Approximately twenty-six percent of the aircraft consisted of the sturdy titanium alloy. Thirty-seven percent was aluminum.

Upon completing the high-speed taxi trials at the St. Louis plant, the first functional Eagle rolled out to a jubilant crowd of McDonnell Douglas employees and contractors in June 1972. A month later, F-1 achieved its first flight on July 27, 1972. McDonnell Douglas test pilot Irving L. Burrows flew the brightly colored F-15 for fifty minutes. Within the following week, another four flights achieved Mach 1.5 and attained an altitude of 45,000.

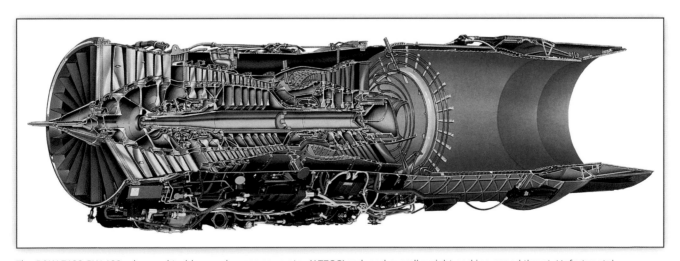

The P&W F100-PW-100 advanced turbine engine gas generator (ATEGG) reduced overall weight and increased thrust. Unfortunately, compressor stalls were a common occurrence and the F100 was eventually replaced with the improved F100-PW-220 engines. The new F100s increased performance using a digital electronic engine control system that produced over 25,000 pounds of thrust to each engine. The upgrade was made standard on all new F-15E models and included in the MSIP F-15 update. *USAF*

Upon flying the F-15, Burrows claimed, "Maneuvering qualities are in excess of anything ordered by our customers. It's a genuine pleasure to suck the Eagle into a turn that leaves any chase airplane staggering around unable to hold either the 'G' or the speed."

For Burrows, the initial flight was nearly problem-free with the exception of a minor landing gear door issue. Flight controls were easier to manage, and inputs resulted in a smoother flight due to the control augmentation system (CAS). The CAS was engineered to provide subtle inputs to aid in the hydro-mechanical flight control system already

place. Designed as a dual-channel, three-axis system, CAS received electronic signals from rudder and stick inputs and managed to filter out unwanted movements such as those caused by turbulence.

The Eagle's flight control system was designed to have a redundant system in the case of structural or mechanical failure. It also aided the pilot through a series of rods and pulleys attached to hydraulic actuators for ease of input. The hydro-mechanical system incorporated a pitch and roll aid to compensate for adverse yaw and roll at supersonic speeds. The pitch-trim compensator solved controlling pitch and trim at supersonic speeds. Variations in speed,

TRIPLE NICKEL

MISSION STATEMENT

To put aircraft, bombs, and missiles precisely on target on time.

HISTORY

The Triple Nickel heritage began on November 25, 1942, when the 555th Bombardment Squadron, Medium, was flying the B-26 Marauder. During World War II, the Nickel led offensive actions against Axis forces from bases in England, France, and Belgium. For gallantry in action, the Nickel was awarded the first of its four Presidential Unit Citations.

the only "Quad Ace" Fighter Squadron, with twenty MiGs to its credit.

In 1968, the Nickel participated in the campaign against the Ho Chi Minh Trail and the Linebacker campaigns against the NVN heartland in 1972. During Linebacker I and II, the Nickel returned to its air superiority role and brought its MiG tally to thirty-nine confirmed victories: ten MiG-17s, three MiG-19s, and twenty-six MiG-21s, producing the first and second USAF aces and earning the motto, "world's largest distributor of MiG parts." From 1966 to 1973, the 555th Tactical

Shortly after World War II ended, Nickel colors were retired as U.S. forces were drawn down. On January 8, 1964, the Nickel re-emerged at MacDill Air Force Base, Florida, with the F-4C Phantom II as its steed. Being the first operational unit in the USAF to receive the Phantom II, the Nickel was deployed and then permanently assigned to the Pacific Rim in support of hostilities in Southeast Asia.

In February 1966, the Nickel returned to combat. Flying out of Udorn Royal Thai Air Base, they scored their first two victories April 23, 1966, and became the first "Ace" Squadron in Southeast Asia with six kills one week later.

In June 1966, the 555th Tactical Fighter Squadron moved to Ubon Royal Thai Air Base, Thailand, and joined the 8th Tactical Fighter Wing, "Wolfpack." There, the squadron led the first strike against MiG airfields in North Vietnam. The Nickel launched the first night bombing attacks against North Vietnam September 29, 1967. While at Ubon, the Nickel downed an additional fourteen aircraft, including four MiG-21s on January 2, 1967. The Nickel was now

Fighter Squadron earned three more Presidential Unit Citations, five Air Force Outstanding Unit awards with combat "V" device, the Republic of Vietnam gallantry cross with palm, and the 1973 Hughes achievement award.

It was the incredible talent of Nickel pilots that led the squadron to historical kill numbers. Such pilots included Maj. Robert A. Lodge (three kills), Capts. Charles B. DeBellevue (six kills), Robert "Steve" Richie (five kills), John A. Madden (three kills), and Roger C. Locher (three kills).

The list of the unit's achievements shows a relentless drive to engage the enemy at his great misfortune. After nine years of distinguished combat operations, the Nickel returned to the United States. In 1974, the squadron moved to Luke Air Force Base, Arizona, where it was again chosen to receive the Air Force's newest fighter, the F-15 Eagle.

On April 1, 1994, the Nickel transferred to Aviano Air Base, Italy, and was honored again by being given the distinction of flying the single seat, supersonic, multi-role 9G F-16C.

This close-up view shows the complex nozzle system originally covered by an aerodynamic network of plates commonly referred to as "Turkey Feathers" or divergent nozzle external segments. High maintenance led to their removal from the nozzle system. This reduced weight by more than one hundred pounds but increased drag by approximately three percent. Use of a convergent exhaust nozzle control motor contracts the nozzle to eighteen inches in diameter. Once afterburn is achieved, the nozzles no longer require a small exit and the diameter expands to its widest aperture. *Tyson V. Rininger*

supersonic and subsonic, as well as sudden weight changes such as dropping fuel tanks or firing missiles, required constant trim adjustments. Although the pilot could manually input trim adjustments via the toggle stick mounted atop the control stick, the pitch-trim compensator would input subtle changes to the angle of the stabilator without requiring the attention of the pilot.

The responsibility of the second completed Eagle F-2 (71-0281) was to provide a test bed for the powerful P&W F100-PW-100 engines. Despite the aforementioned history regarding joint forces development for use in the F-15 and USN F-14 platforms, the F100-PW-100 ATEGG engine continued with production.

As testing proceeded, the engine managed to pass five of its eight scheduled milestones on time despite the increasing cost overruns. As it approached its sixth milestone, the DoD began noticing deficiencies in the motor's compressor section. As long as the engine was able to qualify after reaching the 150-hour endurance test, production for the F100 was granted. The compressor anomaly was addressed once USN participation had completely diminished. The lighter compressor requested by the Navy was simply replaced by a tried and true, albeit heavier, compressor, and the 150-hour endurance test was successfully completed in February 1972.

On September 26, two months after the F-15's first flight, F-2 took to the skies intending to be the

LEFT & ABOVE Testing of this F-15C Eagle, mounted upside down, takes place at what is now Rome Laboratory at Griffiss Air Force Base, New York. A radar warning system pod mounted on the fuselage is tested with the aircraft's onboard radar warning system. Such tests are also conducted on full-scale mockups of an F-35 (JSF), F-16, and F-22. *USAF*

test platform for the F100. Instead, according to Burrows, the F-2 became a "propulsion development vehicle" with two YF100 Series II engines able to produce a rated thrust.

Unfortunately, the F100 was plagued with additional problems forcing military officials to rethink their approach regarding the rigidity of the milestone process. In February 1973, an F100 engine undergoing further endurance testing lost a fan and turbine blade while in the test chamber. Failing the milestone requirement, Brig. Gen. Bellis, F-15 SPO, chose to modify the requirements under authority of the Joint Engine Product Office.

Although Bellis determined the engine failure was based on debris from the test cell and not the engine itself, he modified the milestone requirements. Running the engine at its maximum risked an unrelated failure that might put actual flight testing on hold.

The state-of-the-art Hughes AN/APG-63 radar system was tied into the entire tactical electronic warfare suite (TEWS). Weapons systems, aircraft avionics, and the radar system interacted to provide precise weapons deployment and target elimination along with aircraft survivability. *USAF*

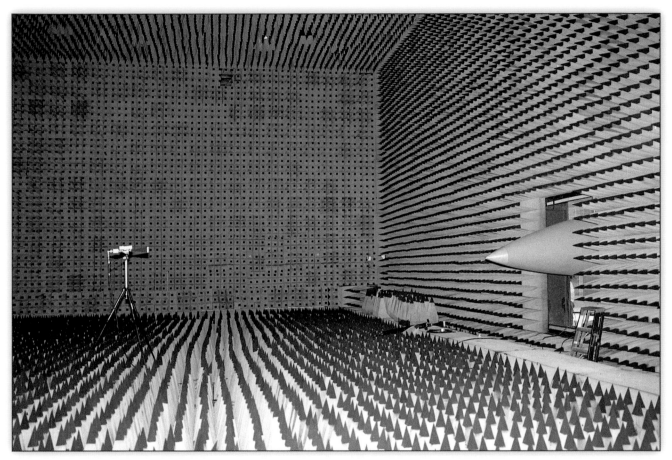

All except the nose of this F-15 is visible. The nose is docked inside the preflight integration of munitions and electronic systems facility, better known as the primes, at Eglin Air Force Base, Florida. During ground tests, the nose is docked and the test aircrew simulates a real dogfight. No other DoD facility simulates moving targets. *USAF*

Although the program's modification proved to be the proper course of action, opponents objected to the changes. With the new regiment, the DoD approved the F100 and issued an FSD five months later than originally proposed. It wasn't until delivery of the secondary engine test bed, or Eagle F-9 (71-0288), that a production model F100-PW-100 was flown.

Problems persisted with on-demand afterburner at medium-altitude, subsonic speeds, along with maintenance crews not having the proper tools and training to service the engines. Although P&W engineers became experts at dealing with engine anomalies and expedient repairs, due to their constant monitoring, proper tooling, and maintenance, techniques were slow to make it to USAF personnel.

Another troublesome feature applied to the engines were the addition of expanding and contracting plates that would overlap covering the external working mechanics of the engine's nozzle. The idea was to blend the flow of air traveling above and below the aircraft with the exhaust flow of the engine. Unfortunately this complex use of plates, also known as "Turkey Feathers," proved to fail more often than not, falling off the aircraft. The decision to discontinue use of the aerodynamic plates and expose the nozzle mechanics, increased drag by three percent.

Hughes Aircraft was busy preparing the "Eyes of the Eagle" in the form of the AN/APG-63 multimode radar system. The radar incorporated the latest in pulse-Doppler technology enabling the F-15 to look up and down, a feature previous radar systems lacked. A big advantage to the pulse-Doppler system was the ability to track enemy aircraft at treetop level by canceling out ground clutter based on the transmitting

The Eagle 76-0116 was the flagship of the 412th Test Wing at Edwards Air Force Base, California. It performed test support for target aircraft, refueling operations, other minor, non-combined test force roles, and was equipped for anti-satellite weapon deployment. Major General Doug Pearson is the only pilot to successfully shoot down a satellite using an air-breathing aircraft in combination with the short-lived anti-satellite weapon program. Flying airframe 76-0084, he fired an ASM-135A missile at the Solwind P78-1 Satellite on September 13, 1985. The F-15A pictured here was retired to the aircraft maintenance and regeneration center at Davis-Monthan Air Force Base in Tucson, Arizona, with Pearson's name still painted on the aircraft. *Tyson V. Rininger*

aircraft's airspeed. Once the radar system acquired the target, it sends the information to the aircraft's central computer where various on-board weapons systems read the data and feed targeting information to the head-up display.

The Eagle's computer system was the most advanced of any fighter ever produced. Although Hughes had the radar technology, IBM designed the backbone of the Eagle's intelligence utilizing its CP-1075/AYK central computer system. The concept enabled one pilot the ability to manage the workload of two, as had been with the F-4 Phantom. The system weighed slightly more than forty-eight pounds and consisted of a high-speed, general-purpose analog computer with a 16.3-kilobyte, 34-bit memory that was expandable to 24.6 kilobytes with a computing speed of 340,000 instructions per second.

Information was translated by the central computer and sent to various screens on the instrument panel in a readable format. The central and most used component was the horizontal situation display (HSI) that can be found today on more technologically advanced general aviation aircraft. Other displays receiving information from the central computer were the HUD, found on the glare shield above the instrument panel and the vertical situation display, located in the upper left portion. Before long, the central computer system within the F-15 was capable of sending information to fourteen separate onboard systems.

Designated "F-3," the Eagle 71-0282 of the Phase I program was to become the first aircraft equipped with the new AN/APG-63 radar. It was the avionics test bed tasked with tackling the symptomatic bugs and glitches all computer systems initially contain. Surprisingly, there were fewer glitches than predicted. The installation of the computer system became one of the most trouble-free aspects of the program.

While the AN/APG-63 provided the "Eyes of the Eagle," the tactical electronic warfare suite (TEWS) provided the ears. Tied into the APG-63, TEWS ultimately consisted of the Loral ALR-56A radar warning receiver, the Northrop ALQ-135 internal countermeasures set, and the Tracor ALE-40/45 countermeasures dispenser, making it the first fully integrated yet independent defensive system incorporated into a fighter. Making its first flight on January 16, 1974, Eagle F-10 (71-0289) was designated as the test bed for the TEWS system and its individual avionics packages.

The ALR-156A radar-warning receiver was responsible for warning pilots of incoming surface-to-air-missiles (SAM) or anti-aircraft artillery (AAA) along with other threats, be they radar installations or other aircraft in the vicinity. The ALQ-135A ICS was activated upon receiving these threats and initialized an electronic form of protection by jamming the signal of the adversary. Jamming signals were sent in all directions via five locations on the airframe: Two rearward facing on top

The TEWS was conveniently placed just behind the pilot of a single-place F-15A. Removal of the TEWS allowed the addition of a second seat. In order for a two-seat F-15B to operate in combat, the TEWS system was replaced with a portable ALQ-119 ECM pod placed on the centerline of the aircraft. Here an AN/ALQ-119 ECM pod is mounted beneath the wing of an F-4E Phantom II aircraft stationed at Osan Air Base with two air-to-surface AGM-65 Maverick missiles attached to its wing pylons. *USAF*

of both vertical stabilizers, two forward facing on both wingtips, and a fifth mounted beneath the forward fuselage. The later C version of the ALQ-135 provided the pilot with the approximate location of the threat viewable in the cockpit TEWS scope.

The ALE-40/45 countermeasures dispenser wasn't initially incorporated into the TEWS package. It would later be added during the multi-stage improvement program (MSIP). Upon acquisition of a hostile weapon, the countermeasures dispenser was used to deploy countermeasure MJU-10 or the brighter and longer lasting MJU-7 flares. It could also dispense metallic chaff designed to confuse weapons' radar units.

Other Eagles to take to the sky as part of the Phase I and Phase II programs were F-4 (71-0283), tasked with structural integrity testing, and F-5 (71-0284), designated the armament test bed equipped with the first M61 gun. Both F-6 and F-7 (71-0285 and 71-0286, respectively) were secondary test platforms expanding upon initial avionics and weapons testing. Eagle F-8 (71-0287) took on high angle of attack and spin testing, as well as fuel systems testing that included air-to-air, refueling studies.

ENGINE CONTROLS AND INDICATORS

ENGINE MASTER SWITCHES

The engine electronic control panel is located near the pilot's right knee toward the front of the side control panel, while the fuel flow start switches are placed at the rearmost position, also on the right-side panel.

Once electrical power has been provided, turning both guarded engine start fuel flow switches on will direct power to the fuel transfer pumps. Each switch directs power to the appropriate FTIT indicator and opens the corresponding airframe mounted engine fuel shutoff valve. The engine master switch must be ON before the corresponding engine can be coupled to the Jet Fuel Start (JFS) as placing the switch in the OFF mode decouples the engine from the JFS. If engine control/essential power is not available, placing an engine master switch OFF will not shut off its airframe mounted engine fuel shutoff valve.

Depending on the ambient temperature or elevation of the aircraft at time of engine start, the Eagle is equipped with an improved series of start fuel flow switches. The switches have positions of HIGH, AUTO, and LOW and are spring loaded to the lever-locked AUTO position.

HIGH: Provides a rich fuel flow for starts and overrides the automatic sequence.

AUTO: Provides a lean fuel flow during normal start. Fuel flow is lean until thirty seconds after the main generator comes on the line then automatically increases 100 pounds per hour (rich).

LOW: Fuel flow will drop approximately 100 pounds per hour when this position is selected.

ENGINE ELECTRONIC CONTROL SWITCHES (F100-PW-100)

The left (L) and right (R) engine electronic control (EEC) switches are located on the engine control panel and provide power to the EEC. The switches have two positions, ON and OFF.

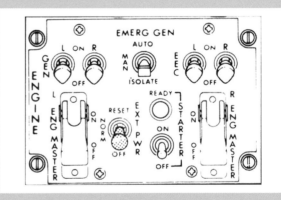

ON: Turns on power to the EEC.

OFF: Turns off ECC supervisory control of UC. Exhaust nozzle remains closed with gear handle down.

JET FUEL STARTER SWITCH

The jet fuel starter (JFS) switch is on the engine control panel located on the right console. It has positions of ON and OFF. During engine start, the JFS is automatically shut down after both engines are started; however, it can be shut down at any time by placing the switch to OFF.

Designed to test the application of trainer two-seat aircraft, McDonnell Douglas incorporated two dual-seat aircraft into the testing regiment. Later dubbed F-15Bs, the two TF-15A aircraft designated TF-1 and TF-2 (71-0290 and 71-0291, respectively) took to the skies on July 7 and October 18, 1973, as two-seat stability and control-test platforms.

Conveniently placed in the rear portion of the cockpit behind the pilot of a single-seat F-15, the internal countermeasures set portion of the TEWS system could easily be removed and a second seat added. Doubling the convenience factor of the internal countermeasures set placement was the ability to free up hardpoints. This made the entire system internal while leaving the two-seat variant a fully functional airframe. To regain the option of an ICS system, a Westinghouse ALQ-119 ECM pod could be placed on the centerline station under the airframe as well as either station one or nine. The TF-15 officially changed to F-15B in December 1977 as a result of combat readiness.

Operational test force pilots had the opportunity in Phase III training to become more acquainted with the capabilities of the aircraft. Pilots took part

JFS READY LIGHT
The JFS ready light is on the engine control panel located on the right console. The light indicates the JFS is ready to be engaged. The light goes out when the JFS shuts down.

GENERATOR CONTROL SWITCHES
Two generator control switches, one for each generator, are on the engine control panel. They are two-position toggle switches with positions of OFF and ON. The switches are lever-lock type and must be raised up before they are moved to a new position.

EMERGENCY GENERATOR CONTROL SWITCH
The emergency generator control switch, on the engine control panel, is a three-position toggle switch with positions of AUTO, MAN, and ISOLATE. The switch is electrically held in the ISOLATE position.

AUTO: Provides automatic activation of the emergency generator if either or both main generators are inoperative, both transformer-rectifiers fail, and either or both main fuel boost pumps fail. After TO 1F-15-764, provides automatic shutdown of the emergency generator thirty seconds after the first main generator comes on the line after a ground start without external power. On all aircraft, for starts with external power, the emergency generator will not operate as long as external power is connected.

MAN: Provides manual activation of the emergency generator.

ISOLATE: Restricts the emergency generator to powering the emergency fuel boost pump and arresting hook and provides power from the emergency/essential 28-volt DC bus to the emergency air refueling switch to open the slipway door. On F-15C 83-0035 and up and F-15D 83-0049 and up, the engine rpm indicators are also powered in this position. In the event of a complete electrical failure, an attempt to restore the emergency generator may be made by cycling the switch to ISOLATE and back to MAN.

EXTERNAL POWER CONTROL SWITCH
The external power control switch on the engine control panel controls application of external power to the aircraft electrical buses. An external power monitor will prevent faulty external power from being connected to the aircraft system.

NORM: Allows the aircraft electrical buses to be energized by external power if no aircraft generators are operating.

RESET: Will establish external power if it is not on the line. It is spring-loaded to NORM.

OFF: Disconnects external power from the aircraft.

ENGINE CONTROL SWITCHES
The engine control switches (not pictured) are present on F-15C/Es equipped with the F100-PW-220 powerplant.

L and R ENG CONTR (engine control): Switches are located on the engine control panel and provide power to the DEEC (digital engine electronic control). The switches have two positions, ON and OFF.

ON: Turns on power to DEEC for normal engine control.

OFF: Turns of DEEC and transfers engine control to secondary mode (hydromechanical). Afterburner inhibited, engine rpm reduced to 80 percent max, and exhaust nozzle will remain closed with gear handle down.

An F-106 Delta Dart aircraft from the 49th Fighter Interceptor Squadron deploys a drogue chute upon landing. To eliminate the time consumed in repacking a chute, an upward extending hydraulic airbrake was installed on the spine of the F-15 and later made larger for faster deceleration. Although the smaller airbrake relieved the aircraft of the cumbersome device, brake temperatures were still of concern in stopping the aircraft. *USAF*

in predetermined Air Force Development, Test and Evaluation exercises reducing potential additional program costs and eventually making it easier to transfer the aircraft to the intended operators. Such exercises engaged dissimilar aircraft such as F-5Es and F-14s that were participating in the USN Top Gun School and utilized the new AN/APG-63 radar system.

Some of the more significant Initial Operational Test and Evaluation exercises consisted of live fire training demonstrations involving the M61A1 Vulcan cannon and various incorporated missile systems. As final proof of the F-15's capabilities to defend against the intended aggressor, the MiG-25 Foxbat, a BOMARC CQM-99B surface-to-air missile was launched to 71,000 feet achieving a speed of Mach 2.7. Although the awaiting F-15 failed to shoot down the target, the proximity of the Sparrow missile was deemed lethal and the test a success. A second test involving the BOMARC missile resulted in complete destruction of the target.

Testing and integration continued, even as the first production aircraft was accepted to an active unit on November 14, 1974. Sporting a large "TAC-1" emblem on the nose, aircraft 73-0108 was delivered to the 555th Tactical Fighter Training Squadron with President Gerald R. Ford in attendance. With testing on schedule, and the Eagle exceeding expectations, the next question was, "Who's going to fly them?"

While the 555th Tactical Fighter Training Squadron, or "Triple Nickel," was accepting aircraft, the unit also served as an interim training facility. It had fighter pilots with F-4 experience whom their unit commanders highly recommended. Upon being certified, the F-4 vets would teach others how to get the most out of the aircraft. It was thought veteran pilots with an F-4 background would be best suited, though when it came time to fill the roles, only the top five percent were chosen. Pilots from TAC, USAFE, and PACAF filled the desired roles.

Pilot training typically began with the Air Training Command headquartered at Randolph Air Force Base,

The 555th Tactical Fighter Training Squadron received the first active duty Eagle (73-108) at Luke Air Force Base in Arizona, with President Gerald Ford in attendance. This air-to-air view shows a flight of five F-15 Eagles flying in an echelon right and high formation. The flagship of the 405th Tactical Training Wing leads the formation, followed by the 426th, 461st, 550th, and 555th Tactical Fighter Training Squadrons. *USAF*

Texas. Flying the T-37 Tweet and T-38 Talon, the first class to pass undergraduate pilot training was at Webb Air Force Base, Texas, in February 1962.

As popular support for the Vietnam War waned and American forces began to pull out of Southeast Asia, the training requirements of Air Training Command (ATC) gradually diminished. From almost 73,000 personnel assigned in 1972, the command shrank to slightly over 50,000 in 1977. President Richard M. Nixon ended the draft on June 30, 1973, converting the military to an all-volunteer force. During this period, the percentage of recruits with a high school education declined to the lowest point in Air Force history. These factors combined to make the 1970s an era of change for ATC.

One change was in the command's approach to technical training. Poor retention rates, and the generally lower quality of recruits, prompted ATC to shift from a career oriented, technical training philosophy to one of teaching only those tasks recruits needed during their first enlistment. This reduced the length of training while also lowering training costs. To supplement on-duty training, and in hopes of attracting higher quality recruits, the USAF established the Community College of the Air Force in 1972 as part of ATC.

In 1974, flight training requirements set forth by ATC consisted of 210 hours total jet flight time over a 45-week period. It was mandated that pilots receive a minimum of 90 hours in the T-37, and 120 hours in the more nimble, and less stable, T-38.

Every pilot had to prove they could handle the Eagle, even the most senior combat veterans who were offered the job. To do so required passing various phases. Once the senior pilots were checked out, the basis for a unit was formed. It was time to bring in first-string lieutenants. Unfortunately, concerns still remained about whether a new pilot fresh out of undergraduate pilot training could handle such a powerful aircraft. Therefore, a special class was devised. Consisting of former F-4 WSOs or F-106

Five F-15 Eagles of the 405th Tactical Training Wing fly past a rock formation rising from the fog-covered floor of Monument Valley. Most Eagle pilots had an F-4 Phantom background and were brought in from TAC, USAF Europe, and the Pacific AF. Once checked out, they became instructors. Students eventually graduated to Langley Air Force Base and, finally, to units based on the front lines in the European and Pacific theaters. *USAF*

pilots, five new lieutenants, and ten F-15 trainees, the military personnel center was pleasantly surprised to see their concerns were unwarranted. Following a proficiency qualification check requiring the pilot to demonstrate knowledge and skill of basic landings, instrument approaches, and formation maneuvering, the pilot was then deemed an Eagle driver and ready to move on to Phase II.

Problems with the Eagle along with the ability to train pilots fast enough became a growing concern. In addition, parts and reliability were causing maintenance and scheduling headaches. The problematic P&W engine was rearing its ugly head with constant failures to light properly. Various components within the aircraft couldn't be replaced in a timely manner due to a lack of readily available spares. Preplanned sorties were almost cut in half reducing the amount of time needed for training. Although it seemed to be creating a black eye for the new aircraft, the "Fighter Mafia" were getting their wish of excluding the ground role from their dream fighter. With the continued reduction in sorties, all air-to-ground training was cancelled in an effort to keep the aircraft's priority service obligation on track.

A flight line crewman directs the first F-15A Eagle aircraft assigned to Langley Air Force Base to a parking spot on the flight line. Pilots were sent to the 1st Tactical Fighter Wing at Langley to learn the Eagle's combat capabilities following their training with the 555th at Luke Air Force Base. *USAF*

Once training had been completed through the 555th, Eagle pilots were off to Langley Air Force Base, Virginia, to join the 1st Tactical Fighter Wing. Since the 1st Fighter Wing had been deactivated in December 1969, Commander in Chief of the Tactical Air Command Gen. William W. "Spike" Momyer sought to revise a unit rich in heritage to assume the Eagle's first command.

General Momyer chose the 15th Tactical Fighter Wing, based at MacDill Air Force Base, Florida, to be redesignated the 1st on July 1, 1971. This effectively made the 45th, 46th, and 47th Tactical Fighter Squadrons the 71st, 27th, and 94th. Less than a year later, he based the technologically advanced fighter at the home of Tactical Air Command headquartered in Langley. His final reasoning for Langley's location was its proximity to Washington, D.C., and the many influential politicians only ninety miles away.

With everything in place, it was the job of Brig. Gen. Larry D. Welch to insure the facilities were prepared to receive the Eagle. To coincide with delivery of the first F-15 along with moving the MacDill unit flag to Langley, a complete infrastructure was needed. It had to include facility construction and maintenance, operational establishment, and a training regiment.

The unique airframe of the F-15A Raw Power (Eagle 77-039) belonged to the 445th Flight Test Squadron at Edwards Air Force Base, California. One of the most powerful F-15As, it was the only A model Eagle that could be powered by either the PW-220 or PW-229 engines. The aircraft was retired and flown to the aircraft maintenance and regeneration center at Davis-Monthan Air Force Base in Tucson, Arizona, on December 10, 2004. *Tyson V. Rininger*

A 33rd Tactical Fighter Wing F-15C Eagle banks into a turn during a flight out of Eglin Air Force Base, Florida. The aircraft is carrying two AIM-9 Sidewinder missiles on each wing and four AIM-120 advanced medium-range air-to-air missiles (AMRAAMs) on its fuselage weapons stations. Although minor development and production glitches were still being worked out of the A model, McDonnell Douglas already had plans for an updated Eagle. The first C model was delivered to Eglin Air Force Base on July 3, 1979. *USAF*

With delivery of the first F-15 (74-0083) on January 9, 1976, the letters "FF" adorned the tail representing the "First Fighter." Some units, especially the F-4-based flights at MacDill didn't take kindly to the new tactical fighter wing and the priority given to Eagle. With slight animosity, F-15 pilots were dubbed "Ego Drivers," and the jet was briefly known as the "Ego Jet."

The 27th Tactical Fighter Squadron Fighting Eagles were the first to receive their jets at a rate of about eight per month, followed by the 71st, Ironmen, in May 1976. As the aircraft arrived, sorties were scheduled to get the new airframes past their IOC. Both units were tasked with completion of Phase II flight requirements. These consisted of performing the duties of a replacement training

unit with up to thirty sorties over a two-and-a-half-month period.

Much of what the new arrivals were taught involved basic flight maneuvering techniques unique to the F-15. Engagements were developed involving one-on-one, one-on-two, and two-on-two utilizing similar and dissimilar aircraft. Following successful engagements against similar airframes, aircraft from other adversarial units such as A-4s and F-4Js from the USN Top Gun School as well as T-38s and F-5Es from the 64th Aggressor Squadron at Nellis Air Force Base participated in dissimilar training exercises. Besides scheduled air combat maneuvering exercises, Eagle pilots were also required to fly air intercept missions along with difficult nighttime air-to-air refueling missions with KC-135 Stratotankers.

Upon completion of Phase II training, pilots were immediately qualified as mission ready, though some modifications had to be made to the program. Difficulties with planning and implementing sorties similar to what the 555th experienced also plagued the 1st Tactical Fighter Wing. In order to get pilots qualified in the most efficient way possible and once the instructor pilot (IP) saw that proficiency had been established, the trainee was offered the chance to complete a check flight enabling him to graduate from Phase II.

As trainees began filtering in from Luke Air Force Base, an increased number of pilot instructors were needed to maintain a steady flow for new units. Upon graduating Phase II, a Mission Ready pilot had the option of becoming an IP by passing a seven-sortie local instructor checkout. Since pilots of the 27th were not dispersed to other units upon reaching mission ready status, the 71st resumed the training regiment enabling the 27th to become the first fully active F-15 unit. Less than two months after receiving their twenty-fourth and final jet, the Fighting Eagles were

1ST TACTICAL FIGHTER WING

As the host unit at Langley Air Force Base, Virginia, the 1st Fighter Wing operates and maintains one of the largest fighter bases in Air Combat Command. The wing flies the F-22A Raptor and F-15 Eagle. The 1st Fighter Wing's mission is to "train, organize and equip expeditionary Airmen; deploy, fight and win; provide world class support to Team Langley."

To accomplish their mission, the men and women of the 1st Fighter Wing work in one of four groups: the Operations Group, Maintenance Group, Mission Support Group, or Medical Group. More than twenty squadrons comprise the four groups. This includes three fighter squadrons: the 27th Fighter Squadron, known as the Fightin' Eagles, the 71st Fighter Squadron, known as the Ironmen, and the 94th Fighter Squadron, known as the Hat-in-the-Ring Gang.

The F-15 Eagle entered operational service at Langley in January 1976, with the 1st Fighter Wing. The wing's current complement of F-15s stands at seventy-five. Continuing the 1st Fighter Wing's tradition of first to bring new fighters operational, the USAF announced in 2002 that the 1st Fighter Wing would become the first F-22A operational wing.

In addition to the F-15 and F-22A, the 1st Fighter Wing has tallied many other firsts throughout its distinguished history. In World War I, when it was known as the 1st Pursuit Organization and Training Center, the wing scored its first aerial victory when Lt. Douglas Campbell of the 94th Fighter Squadron downed a German Phalz D-3 over France. By the time the war ended, the unit's name changed to the 1st Pursuit Group and it earned 202 confirmed kills.

During World War II, the 1st Fighter Wing again excelled, earning three Distinguished Unit Citations for outstanding performance of duty. Redesignated as the 1st Fighter Group, the unit entered the war flying the P-38. Throughout the war, the 1st Fighter Wing flew more than 20,000 sorties on 1,405 combat missions and scored more than 400 aerial kills.

On August 7, 1990, the 1st Fighter Wing, then known as the 1st Tactical Fighter Wing, deployed to Saudi Arabia in support of Operation Desert Shield, adding to the list of firsts by becoming the first U.S. unit to establish air superiority over Saudi Arabia. Through both Operations Desert Shield and Desert Storm, the wing flew more than 6,200 sorties and nearly 25,000 flying hours. The wing also recorded an aerial victory when Capt. Steve Tate of the 71st Fighter Squadron shot down an Iraqi F-1 Mirage.

In 1991, the 1st Tactical Fighter Wing became known, as it is today, as the 1st Fighter Wing. For most of the 1990s, the wing practiced the lessons it learned in operations Desert Shield and Storm by participating in numerous deployments and exercises throughout the world. This practice would pay off.

In 2003, the USAF again called on the 1st Fighter Wing to provide air superiority in combat. The wing deployed to Southwest Asia in support of Operation Iraqi Freedom where it flew over 360 training and combat sorties.

Throughout its history, the 1st Fighter Wing has led the way. On December 15, 2005, the 1st Fighter Wing continued that tradition with the 27th Fighter Squadron, becoming the Air Force's first operational F-22A fighter squadron.

The new F-15C could carry an extra 1,500 gallons of fuel with the use of CFTs and 300 additional gallons internally. Most F-15C units opted not to carry the CFTs because of added drag, but squadrons in remote areas such as Alaska and Greenland routinely made use of the added fuel. *USAF*

deployed to Nellis Air Force Base to participate in the simulated-combat training exercise known as Red Flag on July 6, 1976.

The third element of the 1st Tactical Fighter Wing, the 94th Tactical Fighter Squadron had the most difficulty reaching IOC. The "Hat in the Ring" squadron got the brunt of Eagle delivery problems in addition to being tasked with project Ready Eagle. Under the new project, the 94th was responsible for training USAFE squadrons for overseas deployment at Soesterberg Air Base, Netherlands, and Bitburg Air Base, Federal Republic of Germany. It wasn't until December 1977, seventeen months after receiving their initial Eagle, that the 94th finally achieved IOC.

Soon, a steady flow of Eagles was supplied to the USAF. Additionally, pilots and the training regiment found their rhythm. New units activated at a stable rate. As emphasis on training and maximizing the features of the Eagle increased, the 433rd Fighter Weapons Squadron of the 57th Fighter Weapons

Wing at Nellis Air Force Base began acquiring Eagles to test the limits of CFM and weapons deployment.

Beginning in 1978, the fighter weapons instructor course consisted of a four-month training class involving up to six students. Although the classes were kept extremely small, each graduate left the course with intimate knowledge of the Eagle's weapons systems, aerodynamic principals and enemy engagement tactics. Following the training period, each graduate deployed to a different F-15 unit to share their knowledge with newer F-15 pilots.

Even though the Eagle was still coming into its own, McAir had significant improvements in mind. On July 3, 1979, the first F-15C was delivered to the 60th Tactical Fighter Squadron at Eglin Air Force Base. It was their responsibility to train the PACAF's 18th Tactical Fighter Wing's 67th Tactical Fighter Squadron, Fighting Cocks, to operate the advanced fighter.

Externally, the newer C model was virtually identical to the earlier F-15As. Internal modifications made the F-15C an even more potent aircraft than ever imagined. Fuel capacity was increased internally by 300 gallons and newly developed optional conformal fuel tanks (CFT) further increased capacity by 750 gallons each. Also known as "saddlebags" because of the side-hanging position, CFTs enabled an F-15C to fly for more than five hours at a time.

The only real external difference was made to strengthen the landing gear. With additional fuel capacity came additional weight. Internal support and ribbing was reinforced in order to manage the potential 35,100 pounds of fuel raising the maximum gross weight to 68,000 pounds, 12,000 pounds more than the F-15A. In addition to being heavier, the gear was mounted slightly different to allow for more stability in crosswind landing conditions.

Other improvements included APG-63 radar modifications such as a selectable ground moving target indicator, Doppler beam sharpening, and a Raid assessment mode. The central computer also received upgrades in the form of an overload warning system that monitored maximum G-tolerances to protect the airframe.

Unfortunately, while these improvements were implemented, the P&W F100 engines were only getting worse. Eagles were coming off the assembly line faster than engines and spares could be provided. As the USAF procured Eagles, airframes were shuffled based on engine availability. The biggest problem was the frequency of stall/stagnation incidences.

In the spring of 1979, engine and parts supplies had diminished to the point of being "below zero spares," which effectively meant the USAF had more Eagles than engines. Because F-15s sat in hangars without engines, one could look straight through the entire airframe and see out the other side. This odd phenomenon was coined "holes in aircraft."

The problem stemmed from not realizing the different engine use in an adversarial fighter versus a more gentle constant speed aircraft. When developed, the F100 was designed to 3,350 transient cycles per 1,000 flight hours. A transient cycle is one complete power on to power off motion. As pilots put the Eagle through its paces and aerial warfare it required constant power adjustments. P&W noticed transient cycles numbering over 12,000 per 1,000 flight hours. This meant far greater wear and tear on the components resulting in more frequent teardowns

and rebuilds. It took nearly two years for P&W to catch up by accelerating production of both F100s and their associated parts.

F-15C/D models were soon offered new and improved motors under the Multi Stage Improvement Program (MSIP), upgrading them to the same F100-PW-220 that would eventually find its way onto the F-15E. But MSIP was much larger than just new engines. It was a program that would bring the Eagle out of the analog world and into digital.

The PW-220 was slightly less powerful than the PW-100, but the benefits of the digital electronic engine control far outweighed the 380 pounds less thrust. The digital electronic engine control system allowed the pilot to run the engine through multiple cycles with less wear and tear. Digitally controlled, the engine was able to monitor itself constantly for best performance and greater efficiency based on optimum power curves for the desired output. The digital electronic engine control system also enabled the pilot faster response time for enhanced maneuverability and more instantaneous afterburner ignition.

Initially, the MSIP program was divided into two stages; MSIP I was to enhance the warfighting capabilities of the F-15A/B models and MSIP II concentrated on the F-15C/D platforms. Early F-15 models were upgraded through a relatively restricted program designed to bring the airframes and electronics to current but basic technology. The MSIP II programs were escalated to provide active duty Eagles with the most advanced technology available both at the depot level and at the St. Louis production facility. Due to the expense of having two separate programs, MSIP I was eventually merged with MSIP II. Both were simply referred to as the MSIP program.

In response to newly introduced advanced weaponry such as the Advanced Medium-Range Air-to-Air Missile (AMRAAM), the F-15 also needed upgrades. In addition, the inclusion of the Su-27 Flanker and the MiG-29 Fulcrum to the Soviet forces required enhancing the Eagle to defend against the new threats. Areas of concentration for the MSIP program included updating the central computer from analog to digital, modifying the hands-on throttle and stick (HOTAS) for easier use, and enabling the Eagle future use of the Link 16 data link system.

An F-15A Eagle undergoes a multi-stage improvement program (MSIP) upgrade at the Warner Robins Air Logistics Center in Georgia. The MSIP program reinvigorated the aging F-15A/Bs and analog F-15C/Ds and brought them into the digital world. Other aircraft enhancements included improved radar and cockpit management. Most important, the upgraded digital electronic engine control (DEEC) PW-220 powerplant replaced the problematic PW-100. *USAF*

Requiring an estimated 10,000 man-hours to complete, the modification kits were installed around planned depot maintenance schedules mainly at the Warner-Robins Air Logistics Center in Georgia. Kits consisted of twenty-nine separate configurations, including forty-eight sub-kits with nine support equipment kits and ten commodity class kits per airframe scheduled for upgrade.

In order to support the new AMRAAM, the Eagle's MUX system received the faster MIL-STD-1760 interface unit required to transfer data between the aircraft and weapon. The new interface also enabled the use of a very-high-speed integrated circuit, central computer, giving the Eagle greater memory capacity and improved computer-processing speed.

Other modifications included a revised control stick and throttle quadrant providing two additional multi-function switches on each. The new stick controls allowed for better radar control and an automatic acquisition switch. The throttle was equipped with a two-way missile reject switch and an advanced multi-function switch. These gave the pilot better control of the Eagle's electronic identification systems operation and allowed the pilot to initiate combined interrogations.

All Eagles S/N 84-001 came with MSIP modifications already installed. A total of 427 F-15s would eventually receive the avionics upgrade providing them with "maximum air superiority in a dense hostile environment."

Later the F-15Cs received the $200,000 Link 16 data-link upgrade. In combination with the new helmet-mounted cueing system, tests showed a five-fold increase in air-to-air kill ratios. This eventually proved to be the most advanced addition to aerial supremacy since the inclusion of radar according to the 1999 House Appropriations Defense Committee.

LEFT This F-15A Eagle is overhauled as part of the MSIP. Improvements to the avionics and weapons systems consisted of twenty-nine separate configurations, including forty-eight sub-kits with nine support equipment kits and ten commodity class kits per airframe. Additional modifications included the hands-on throttle and stick (HOTAS) system, a provision for the future, Link-16 data link system, and the new, very high speed integrated-circuit central computer. Each aircraft upgrade saw an estimated 10,000 man-hours investment. *USAF*

Airframe 85-0102 launches from Nellis Air Force Base in Las Vegas, Nevada, as part of a Red Flag exercise. During Operation Desert Storm, Capt. David Rose downed a MiG-23 and Capt. Anthony R. Murphy shot down two Su-22s. Both pilots utilized this airframe and the AIM-7M Sparrow missile. The Eagle is now the flagship for the 58th Tactical Fighter Squadron, based at Eglin Air Force Base, with "Gulf Spirit" proudly displayed on the nose. The close-up shows the Su-7 shot down by Col. Rick Parson on February 7, 1991, using airframe 84-0124. *Tyson V. Rininger (take-off photo); USAF (close-up photo)*

CHAPTER THREE

F-15 AT WAR

WITH THE COLD WAR IN ITS PRIME, EAGLES were quickly sent to the front lines at bases all around the world. Units in Japan, Europe, and Alaska patrolled all facets of communist-controlled countries as well as defending the borders of allied nations. As intended, the Eagle became America's frontline fighter. The Eagle's impervious combat record proved its ferocity in the field not only with the USAF, but its allied customers.

The 36th TFW at Bitburg, Federal Republic of Germany (FRG), was the first to receive the F-15 outside the continental United States. Since intelligence reports were showing a large increase in Foxbats and Floggers stationed at German Democratic Republic, Czechoslovakian, and Polish bases, it seemed the European front would be the most likely arena for a Cold War show of force.

Maintenance personnel meet an F-15 Eagle from the 53rd Tactical Fighter Squadron, 36th Tactical Fighter Wing, at Bitburg Air Base, after a mission over Bosnia to enforce the no-fly zone. The 36th was the first wing to receive the Eagle for action on the front line. Eagles from Bitburg performed peacetime air policing as well as wartime air defense and air superiority. *USAF*

RIGHT Brigadier General Frederick C. Kyler, commander of the 36th Tactical Fighter Wing, sits in the cockpit of an F-15A Eagle after completing a flight. Stationed in Bitburg, Germany, Kyler was the first to command an active unit participating in Cold War exercises. *USAF*

BELOW This TFS F-15C Eagle carries a full load of AIM-9 Sidewinder and AIM-7 Sparrow missiles during a Zulu alert mission designed to protect northern NATO nations from possible attack. The 32nd Tactical Fighter Squadron is the only USAF squadron to bear the official crest of the Queen of the Netherlands on the side of its F-15C fighter. *USAF*

Flying nonstop to Bitburg AB, two F-15Bs touched down on January 7, 1977, followed by 522 mission capable maintainers at the ready by April of that year. The two aircraft, (75-0049 and 75-0050) were to become maintenance trainers in preparation for the arrival of the rest of the unit.

Being the first unit to potentially experience conflict, it was imperative that Eagle pilots be properly trained for combat. Because of this threat, the 36th Tactical Fighter Wing ("Bulldogs"), under command of Brig. Gen. Fred Kyler, was the first F-15 unit to actively participate in a Red Flag combat training

Lieutenant Colonel Ray Klosowski, 179th Fighter Interceptor Squadron, maps out flight plans during Creek Klaxon. Air National Guard units from twenty states temporarily assumed the Zulu Alert duties of the 526th as part of the exercise at Ramstein Air Base, Germany. Flying F-4 Phantoms, the 526th and 512th Tactical Fighter Squadrons, under the 86th Tactical Fighter Wing, assisted the Bitburg-based F-15As with patrolling the Federal Republic of Germany. *USAF*

A pair of Bitburg Eagles always remained cocked and ready for launch in the event of an Alpha or Tango alert. Tango alerts consisted of routine training missions intended to test the IADS system and aircrew. Alpha alerts were real scrambles. They usually called for an interception of wayward aircraft. *USAF*

exercise prior to deployment. With the assistance of nine KC-135s, twenty-three F-15s were finally on the ground in the USAFE theater by April 27, 1977.

Earlier aircraft such as the Sabre and Super Sabre had range limitations meaning an increased number of bases to assist the Allied Tactical Air Force (ATAF).

The addition of the F-15 with its more efficient powerplant and greater range meant fewer bases were needed to perform the required tasks. The missions assumed by the 36th Tactical Fighter Wing included peacetime air policing of NATO as well as air defense and air superiority during wartime. With Bitburg's central location, the new Eagles fit perfectly within NATO's newly structured central region Integrated Air Defense System (IADS).

In combination with the two F-4E squadrons of the 86th Tactical Fighter Wing out of Ramstein AB, the American-led Allied Tactical Air Force (4ATAF) and the British-run 2ATAF, consisting of forces from five separate nations, combined to make up part of the Allied Air Forces Central Europe (AAFCE). The 2ATAF was responsible for patrolling and protecting the northern portion of FRG while the 4ATAF defended the southern FRG.

A certain number of Eagles in the USAFE theater were always armed and on alert. Typically, it was the responsibility of two pilots from each element of a different squadron to see that the jets were armed and ready for flight at a moment's notice for a twenty-four-hour period. This was known as "being cocked." Of the three available units, the on-alert squadron would stand up for a period of one month, assume the standby position the following month, and be off-duty for the third month.

When called to action, pilots were faced with two types of scrambles, an "Alpha" or a "Tango." Alpha

An F-15C Eagle from the 12th Fighter Squadron, Elmendorf Air Force Base, intercepts a Russian Tu-95 Bear bomber during a Russian military exercise near the western coast of Alaska. The North American Aerospace Defense Command launched three pairs of fighters to detect, intercept, and identify the aircraft. It was a fairly routine event as Bears typically flew from Siberia and over the North Pole for Northern Pacific patrol missions. Captain Anthony Schiavi, 58th Tactical Fighter Squadron, flew Eagle 85-0104, shown in this photograph, when he shot down a MiG-23 during Operation Desert Storm. *USAF*

U.S. AIR FORCES EUROPE (USAFE)

MISSION

As the air component for U.S. EUCOM, USAFE directs air operations in a massive theater. The area spans three continents, covers more than twenty million square miles, contains ninety-one countries, possesses one-fourth of the world's population, and holds about one-third of the world's gross domestic product.

During the Cold War, USAFE was a fight-in-place force postured for a large-scale conflict. Since the fall of the Berlin Wall, it has transitioned to an Air Expeditionary Force with a mobile and deployable mix of people and resources that can simultaneously operate in multiple locations. Its role in Europe and Africa has included warfighting as well as humanitarian and peacekeeping operations and other non-traditional contingencies throughout its area of responsibility.

In peacetime, USAFE trains and equips U.S. Air Force units pledged to NATO. In fulfilling its NATO responsibilities, USAFE maintains combat-ready wings based from Great Britain to Turkey. USAFE plans, conducts, controls, coordinates, and supports air and space operations in Europe, Asia, and Africa to achieve U.S. national and NATO objectives based on taskings by the U.S. EUCOM commander.

In support of national and NATO requirements, USAFE assets stand ready to perform close air support, air interdiction, air defense, in-flight refueling, long-range transport, and support of maritime operations. USAFE remains a formidable force despite a rapid drawdown that saw its main operating bases cut by sixty-seven percent following the end of the Cold War. As witnessed in the command's support of contingency and humanitarian operations throughout Europe and parts of Africa, USAFE remains a highly responsive and capable combat force.

PERSONNEL AND RESOURCES

More than 39,000 active-duty Reserve Air National Guard and civilian employees are assigned to USAFE. Equipment assets include

about 220 fighter, attack, rotary wing, tanker, and transport aircraft and a full complement of conventional weapons.

ORGANIZATION

USAFE consists of seven main operating bases along with seventy geographically separated locations. The main operating bases are: RAF Lakenheath and Mildenhall in England, Ramstein and Spangdahlem Air Bases in Germany, Aviano Air Base in Italy, Lajes Air Base in the Azores, and Incirlik Air Base in Turkey. These bases report to Third Air Force (Air Forces Europe) located at Ramstein Air Base, for day-to-day and contingency operations. Third Air Force (Air Forces Europe) is USAFE's Component Numbered Air Force responsible for maintaining a continuous, theater-wide, situational awareness and providing the Commander, Air Force Forces, the capability to command and control assigned and attached forces.

HISTORY

USAFE originated as the 8th Air Force in 1942 and flew heavy bombardment missions over the European continent during World War II. In August 1945, the command was given its current name, U.S. Air Forces in Europe. At that time, USAFE had 17,000 airplanes and 450,000 people.

During the Berlin Airlift from 1948 to 1949, USAFE airlifted more than 1.6 million tons of food, fuel, and medical supplies to the blockaded city. With the formation of NATO in 1949, the United States was committed to help defend Western Europe against aggression from the Soviet Union, a mission that continued until the fall of the Berlin Wall in 1989.

In March 1973, Headquarters USAFE transferred from Lindsey Air Station, Wiesbaden, West Germany, to Ramstein Air Base. In the mid-1980s, USAFE maintained and operated twenty-five main bases and more than 400 geographically separated units in 190

scrambles were intended to intercept wayward aircraft or unknown radar returns and were considered actual launches. Tango alerts were training scrambles designed to test the flight crew and aircraft handlers as well as the entire IADS. It was common for aircraft to be launched to a low-fly area for simulated bombing

and ordinance delivery runs, though never in an armed aircraft.

Codenamed "Zulu," a pair of Bitburg Eagles always remained cocked and ready to scramble at a moment's notice. Each morning, a pair of pilots and their maintainers would run through the aircraft

different locations. These bases supported about 850 aircraft. The community stood at more than 140,000: 60,000 active-duty airmen, 10,000 civilian workers, and almost 70,000 family members.

Beginning in late 1990, USAFE mobilized and moved more than 180 aircraft and 5,400 people to the Persian Gulf area in support of Operations Desert Shield and Desert Storm. In addition, 100 aircraft and 2,600 personnel deployed to Turkey for Operation Proven Force, which denied the Iraqis a safe haven for their military forces in northern Iraq. USAFE also activated aeromedical staging facilities and contingency hospitals. More than 9,000 patients, mostly suffering from non-combat-related illnesses and injuries, were evacuated to Europe and more than 3,000 were treated at USAFE medical facilities.

After Desert Storm, USAFE provided emergency relief to Kurdish refugees fleeing Iraqi forces and enforced a no-fly zone over northern Iraq. This mission, known first as Operation Provide Comfort and later as Operation Northern Watch, continued until March 2003.

Since 1990, USAFE has handled more than seventy contingencies, more than twice as many in the 1970s and 1980s combined. For example, the command took part in Operation Provide Hope I and II, which airlifted food and medical supplies to the people of the former Soviet Union, and Provide Promise, the airlifting of supplies into war-torn Yugoslavia from July 1992 until December 1995.

USAFE also provided air protection over the skies of Bosnia-Herzegovina in Operation Deny Flight. Along with allies from NATO countries, USAFE aircrews applied airpower in Operation Deliberate Force, the bombing campaign that paved the way for the Dayton Peace Agreement. USAFE then helped deploy Peace Implementation Forces and equipment to Bosnia for Operation Joint Endeavor and sustained them by airlift.

USAFE forces again mobilized in March 1999, when NATO intervened in Kosovo to stop Serb repression of the province's ethnic Albanian majority. Efforts to find a diplomatic solution collapsed, resulting in Operation Allied Force, the NATO-led air war over Kosovo. The seventy-eight-day operation ended June 10, culminating in the withdrawal of Serb forces from Kosovo and the eventual return of refugees to their homeland. USAFE's 3rd Air Force led Joint Task Force Shining Hope, established to assist the hundreds of thousands of refugees expelled from Kosovo by Serb soldiers and paramilitaries. USAFE continues to contribute to NATO-led forces promoting peace and stability in Kosovo.

In February 2000, USAFE forces again responded to a humanitarian crisis, this time in southern Africa. Joint Task Force Atlas Response was established to airlift aid to victims of massive floods in Mozambique and other nearby countries. Working with international relief agencies, U.S. forces assisted with a variety of humanitarian-related activities, including the airlift of food and medical supplies, aerial surveillance, and rescue operations in the region.

USAFE has been in the frontlines of the war on terrorism since September 11, 2001. During Operation Enduring Freedom, it supported an air bridge from Europe to Asia that delivered 3,300 tons of humanitarian daily rations to northern Afghanistan, opened a base in Kyrgystan for coalition forces, and established a medical evacuation network that moved nearly 4,000 patients. USAFE deployed twenty-four fighter aircraft, eight KC-135 tankers, and nearly 2,400 people in Operation Iraqi Freedom. It opened an important airfield in northern Iraq and provided critical, en route support to deploying forces, not to mention vital logistical and medical support to forward-deployed forces.

Today, USAFE airmen are engaged in a wide range of active U.S. military efforts in Europe and Africa, including realistic U.S. and NATO exercises and the war on terrorism. The command also plays a major role in furthering democracy in the former Eastern Bloc, as USAFE people take part in Partnership for Peace exercises and Military-to-Military contact programs. In July 2006, USAFE also supported the departure of nearly 15,000 American citizens from Lebanon following the outbreak of hostilities between Lebanese Hizbollah and Israeli Defense Forces in southern Lebanon.

USAFE averaged more than 1,500 deployed to the U.S. Central Command's area of responsibility in 2006. More than three thousand are deployed in support of the war on terrorism and Iraqi Freedom. USAFE also hosted an average of three hundred ANG and more than one thousand, active-duty personnel to the USEUCOM's AOR in 2006.

readiness checklist. This consisted of starting the jet and running through the various computer systems to ensure everything was programmed appropriately for a potential scramble. They also tested missile and computer communications along with the inertial navigation system. Finally, the crew preset all radio frequencies for the appropriate ground and tower communications.

While Eagles were protecting friendly forces in Europe, points closest to the U.S. in proximity to Soviet soil needed to be protected as well. Soviet bases in Siberia routinely sent Tu-95 Bears over the

Pole into U.S. airspace via Alaska. Aircraft from the Alaskan Air Command, part of the Pacific Air Force (PACAF), would scramble to intercept.

The first unit to receive the Eagle was the 43rd Tactical Fighter Squadron, part of the 21st Composite Wing that maintained alert stations in Eielson, Elmendorf, Galena and King Salmon Air Force Base. In November 1982, two King Salmon Air Force Base F-15s intercepted a Soviet Tu-95KM for the first time.

The 43rd Tactical Fighter Squadron was responsible for patrolling over 580,000 square miles from the North Pole to the tip of the Aleutian Islands. To relieve some of the responsibility, the 54th Tactical Fighter Squadron with newer F-15C models joined the 43rd on May 8, 1987. Following a designation change from the 21st Control Wing to the 3rd Wing, aircraft of other types soon joined the far northwest, including two Boeing E-3B AWACS (airborne warning and control system) aircraft, twenty-one F-15Es, eighteen Lockheed C-130Hs, and three C-12F/J liaison and communication aircraft.

Besides Alaska, the northernmost unit protecting the contiguous forty-eight states was the 318th Fighter

In a slightly awkward encounter over a once heavily protected area, three F-15 Eagles from the 21st Tactical Fighter Wing escort two Soviet MiG-29s to Elmendorf Air Force Base for refueling. They flew on to British Columbia and Salinas, California, as part of a friendship tour performing at air shows throughout North America. *USAF*

Two MiG-29 aircraft are intercepted by F-15 Eagles of the 21st Composite Fighter Wing. The 43rd and 54th Tactical Fighter Squadrons, part of the 21st CFW, patrolled 580,000 square miles from the North Pole to the tip of the Aleutian Islands. *USAF*

Intercept Squadron. Operated as part of the Air Defense Command (which would later become the Air Defense Tactical Air Command), the 318th's primary mission was remaining on air defense alert should there be an intercontinental ballistic missile (ICBM) attack from a Soviet location. Besides operating out of McChord Air Force Base in Pierce County, Washington, the 318th also maintained an alert detachment at Castle Air Force Base in Central California.

In addition to the 318th, the 5th Fighter Interceptor Squadron was based out of Minot Air Force Base, North Dakota, in defense of the newer cruise missile technology. With the introduction of the supersonic Tu-22M Backfire, Soviet forces were able to fly over the North Pole across Canadian soil and launch a series of AS-4 Kitchen nuclear cruise missiles. Because of the threat, the 318th routinely launched practice sorties, honing in on small radar-cross-section targets.

In the northeast, the 57th Fighter Interceptor Squadron located at Keflavik, Iceland, provided protection. This was an effort to patrol the Soviet highway routinely traveled by long-range attack bombers and maritime reconnaissance aircraft. Originally, Iceland refused foreign military involvement on its soil even after joining NATO in 1949. However, due to the development of long-range Soviet nuclear bombers, Iceland modified its policy in 1951.

Soviet Tu-95 Bears routinely traveled through the Greenland, Iceland, and United Kingdom gap to patrol the waters of the North Atlantic. Departing from bases like Murmansk and Archangel, it was common for Bears to monitor shipping and NATO activities while on route to Cuba. To reach their destination, Soviet fighters were forced to fly through a small gap between Greenland and the United Kingdom, almost directly above Keflavik Air Base.

Far from the chilly waters of Alaska and Iceland, the Hawaii Air National Guard (HIANG) patrols the most isolated islands in the world. The 199th Tactical Fighter Squadron, better known as the "HANGmen," a play on the HIANG acronym, have some of the highest-time Eagle pilots in the Air National Guard. *USAF*

The 57th received C model Eagles as their first jets of that type in November 1985. Previously, the Black Knights operated F-102s, F-4Cs, and F-4Es, but the Eagles were different than other units. Upon arrival, the F-15s were already equipped with CFTs and became one of the only C units to regularly fly with them attached. The added 1,500 gallons of fuel enabled the Eagles to intercept Bears at a much further distance and remain on station with them for a longer period of time. After getting accustomed to the CFTs and being one of the only units to use them regularly, the girthy 57th came to be known as flying the "Wide Bodies." In a thirty-year period from 1962 to 1991, the 57th managed to intercept more than three thousand Soviet aircraft.

The 1990s tested the F-15's abilities. By the start of Operation Desert Shield, the F-15C and E were in their prime and ready for the battlefield. On August 2,

1990, Iraqi forces invaded Kuwait with little resistance to their surprise attack. Immediately, F-15s from the 1st Tactical Fighter Wing deployed to protect against a possible invasion of Saudi Arabia.

In less than a week, fifty-two 1st Tactical Fighter Wing F-15s performed combat air patrols (CAPs) along the border of Saudi Arabia and Iraq. While coalition forces amassed, Iraq continued its occupation of Kuwait, claiming historical ownership of the land. Under the moniker "Operation Desert Shield," an allied coalition formed to protect surrounding nations from invasion. Once prepared and ready, coalition forces began Operation Desert Storm flushing the Iraqi troops out of Kuwait and destroying much of their military infrastructure.

Operation Desert Storm began on January 17, 1991, when coalition forces invaded Kuwait at the order of President George W. Bush Sr. Coalition pilots faced moderately trained Iraqi Air Force (IRAF) pilots in MiG-21 Fishbeds, MiG-23ML and MiG-23MS/MF Floggers, MiG-25PD Foxbats, and the extremely agile MiG-29 Fulcrum.

Aircraft units flew predetermined sorties mapped out for maximum effect in taking out Iraqi IADSs as well as runways, grounded aircraft, and command, control, and communications positions. This pre-planned map of sorties was known as the "air tasking order" or "frag" (short for "fragmentary order").

Most Eagles provided aerial support for bombers, tankers, and AWACS aircraft as well as CAP for allied protection, though mainly from the south. As Eagles began to operate out of Turkey, northern CAP missions became more prevalent. Eagles found themselves flying mixed offense and defense missions simultaneously.

Eagle units often switched between offensive and defensive roles. Offensive counter air missions required F-15s to fly deep into Iraqi airspace looking

Freshly painted Eagles from the 18th Tactical Fighter Wing adorn the flight line at Kadena Air Base in Japan. Maintenance personnel and flight crews preflight some of the squadron's F-15s during exercise Giant Warrior 1989. Even though Japan operated a fleet of F-15Js, the United States patrolled the waters off communist China and provided additional protection for the Japanese Air Self Defense Force. *USAF*

U.S. AIR FORCE PACIFIC (PACAF)

MISSION

PACAF's primary mission is to provide ready air and space power to promote U.S. interests in the Asia-Pacific region during peacetime, through crisis, and in war.

The command's vision is to be the most respected air warrior team employing the full spectrum of air and space power, with our Asia-Pacific partners, to ensure peace and advance freedom.

PACAF's area of responsibility extends from the west coast of the United States to the east coast of Africa and from the Arctic to the Antarctic, more than one hundred million square miles. The area is home to nearly two billion people who live in forty-four countries. PACAF maintains a forward presence to help ensure stability in the region.

PERSONNEL AND RESOURCES

The command has approximately forty-five thousand military and civilian personnel serving in nine major locations and numerous smaller facilities, primarily in Hawaii, Alaska, Japan, Guam, and South Korea. Approximately three hundred fighter and attack aircraft are assigned to the command.

ORGANIZATION

PACAF's major units are: 5th Air Force, Yokota Air Base, Japan; 7th Air Force, Osan Air Base, South Korea; 11th Air Force, Elmendorf Air Force Base, Alaska; and 13th Air Force, Andersen Air Force Base, Guam.

Major units also include: 3rd Wing, Elmendorf Air Force Base; 8th Fighter Wing, Kunsan Air Base, South Korea; 15th Air Base Wing, Hickam Air Force Base; 18th Wing, Kadena Air Base, Japan (Okinawa); 51st Wing, Osan Air Base; 343rd Wing, Eielson Air Force Base, Alaska; 35th Fighter Wing, Misawa Air Base, Japan; 374th Airlift Wing, Yokota Air Base; and the 36th Air Base Wing, Andersen Air Force Base.

HISTORY

PACAF traces its roots to the activation of Far East Air Forces, August 3, 1944, at Brisbane, Queensland, Australia. FEAF was subordinate to the U.S. Army Forces Far East and served as the headquarters of Allied Air Forces Southwest Pacific Area. By 1945, three numbered air forces, 5th, 7th, and 13th, were supporting operations in the Pacific. At that time, the Army Air Forces in the Pacific became part of the largest and most powerful military organization ever fielded by any country in the world.

After World War II, FEAF and 5th Air Force remained in Japan, while 7th Air Force operated from Hawaii, and 13th Air Force from the Philippines. In the postwar years, FEAF was designated the theater air force for the Far East Command. All air forces in

for enemy fighters. Defensive units remained with surveillance aircraft or larger bombers.

The Eagle's first combat kill came in the early morning hours of the first day of the war. Colonel Jon "JB" Kelk flying with the 58th Tactical Fighter Squadron, engaged and downed a MiG-29. Almost immediately afterward, Capt. Robert "Cheese" Graeter scored the first double-kill by taking down two Mirage F1EQs. A total of six enemy aircraft were shot down on January 17. This was repeated two days later with another six kills in one day by F-15 Eagles.

On that day, Eagles shot down two MiG-25 Foxbats, the very aircraft that instigated the development of the F-15. In addition, Eagles eliminated two MiG-29

Fulcrums and two Mirage F1EQs from the possible threat of further attacks.

One of the most successful sorties took place on January 27, 1991, when pilots Capt. Jay Denney and Capt. Ben "Coma" Powell shot down four aircraft. Despite that most IRAF aircraft and supporting infrastructure were believed to be suppressed, the two F-15 pilots engaged three MiG-23s and a Mirage F1EQ. By the end of the ordeal, the two Eagle pilots each claimed two victories.

Almost two weeks later, on February 6, 1991, two Eagles of the 53rd Tactical Fighter Squadron based at Bitburg, FRG, repeated the feat. Captain Thomas Dietz engaged and shot down two MiG-21s with two simultaneously fired, AIM-9 Sparrows, while Lt. Bob

the Far East and Southwest Pacific were placed under one Air Force commander for the first time.

When the North Koreans crossed the 38th parallel June 25, 1950, FEAF consisted of 5th Air Force, 13th Air Force, 20th Air Force, and the Far East Materiel Command. Four years after the Korean War armistice, FEAF was redesignated Pacific Air Forces and transferred its headquarters to Hickam.

By 1960, PACAF maintained a combat-ready deterrent force of some thirty-five squadrons, operating from ten major bases in half-dozen countries. In the early 1960s communist military strength and firepower in Vietnam increased. As a result, PACAF began a buildup in the area with the addition of troops and better arms and equipment.

Combat aircraft of PACAF flew their last strikes in Cambodia August 15, 1973, writing the final chapter to the long and costly history of active American participation in the Indochina War. The post-Vietnam era found the command focusing on improving its readiness.

PACAF's organizational structure saw a marked period of rapid and extensive changes. Andersen was reassigned from Strategic Air Command in 1989, and 11th Air Force became a part of the command in late 1990. Following the volcanic eruption of Mount Pinatubo, Clark Air Base, the Philippines, was closed and 13th Air Force relocated to Andersen in 1991.

In 1992, changes took place in force structure within PACAF as the command assumed control of theater-based, tactical airlift wings, theater C-130 aircraft and crews, and associated theater C-130 support. PACAF also gained control of all operational support aircraft and all aeromedical airlift assets in the Pacific.

Throughout its history PACAF has played a vital role in world events. In addition to its key combat role in World War II, Korea, and Vietnam, PACAF units fought in Desert Storm in 1991, and they continue to deploy to Saudi Arabia, Turkey, and Italy for peacekeeping operations. PACAF provided its expertise, aircraft, personnel, and equipment to facilitate the new Expeditionary Air Force, especially as it applied to successful air bridge operations spanning the vast Pacific Ocean. Following the September 11, 2001, terrorist attacks on the United States; PACAF again demonstrated its intrepid spirit through its units deployed in support of Operations Noble Eagle and Enduring Freedom.

Since 1944, the command has participated in more than 140 humanitarian operations within its area of responsibility and beyond. In these operations, PACAF people quickly and efficiently airlifted food, medicine, and other supplies to areas devastated by storms, floods, earthquakes, volcanoes, and other natural disasters.

Additionally, the command supported three of the largest evacuations ever undertaken by the Air Force. These included the Newlife evacuation of Vietnamese in 1975; the Fiery Vigil evacuation of Clark Air Base, Philippines, after the 1991 volcanic eruption of Mount Pinatubo; and the Pacific Haven operation to support and resettle Kurdish evacuees in 1997.

For more than five decades PACAF has served in defense of the nation. The command continually prepares to bring air power quickly and decisively to the far reaches of the Pacific.

Hehemann targeted two Su-25s and eliminated them with AIM-9s.

During the course of Operation Desert Storm, USAF F-15 Eagles shot down thirty-four IRAF aircraft. In addition, Royal Saudi Air Force (RSAF) F-15Cs shot down an additional two IRAF planes. At the end of the war, F-15s tallied thirty-six kills and zero losses. The F-15s could rightly claim "aerial superiority."

Following Operation Desert Storm, Operation Northern Watch (ONW) and Operation Southern Watch (OSW) ensued. These operations were designed to control the areas north of the 36th Parallel and south of the 32nd whereby coalition aircraft would patrol the Iraqi no-fly zones (NFZ). In 1996, the southern NFZ expanded to the 33rd Parallel. The objective of the NFZs was to prevent Saddam Hussein's military from attacking humanitarian efforts toward the Kurdish minority in the north and the Shi'ite population to the south.

Eagles tasked with supporting OSW were mainly based out of Riyadh, Saudi Arabia, although some units were also launched out of Kuwait, Oman, and additional surrounding countries. With RAF (Royal Air Force-UK) Nimrods and USAF E-3 AWACS supplying intelligence support, F-15Cs were tasked with engaging IRAF violators. In addition, the Eagles were to provide protective escort for attack aircraft, tankers, and early warning electronics aircraft in the area. In the meantime, F-15E Strike Eagles were receiving the brunt of the attack missions by removing ground threats and slowly disassembling the Iraqi Army by force.

Operation Northern Watch was a result of Operation Provide Comfort, an effort to assist the Kurdish people in moving north to avoid Saddam Hussein's regime. Enforcing the NFZ meant protecting ground convoys delivering food and supplies as well as NATO-operated C-130 Hercules aircraft.

Most F-15Cs flying ONW were based at Incirlik, Turkey. They launched in limited numbers due to the host country's stipulations. The long flights to the NFZ and back required multiple tankings resulting in five- to six-hour missions or longer.

Another NFZ was established over the country of Bosnia-Herzegovina in October 1992, Established by the UN Security Council's Resolution 781, Operation Deny Flight protected UN Forces assisting humanitarian efforts in Bosnia and Herzegovina from attacks by Serbia and Montenegro. Two years after the implementation of Operation Deny Flight, diplomatic efforts became strained resulting in NATO attacks on Serbian targets located throughout Croatia. Prior engagements hinting to the foreseeable unrest included USAF F-16s shooting down four Serbian SOKO G-4 Super Galeb aircraft violating the NFZ.

These actions made way for Operation Deliberate Force in which NATO aircraft were called to attack Serbian threats near Sarajevo on August 30, 1995. Limited attacks under the guise of both operations required F-15Cs to provide protection to NATO aircraft.

After Yugoslavian President Slobodan Milosevic ignored warnings for the removal of armed forces from Kosovo, NATO instituted Operation Allied Force

U.S. Air Force maintenance technicians deployed to the 363rd Expeditionary Maintenance Squadron prepare an F-15C Eagle for a mission in a sandstorm. The Iraqi Air Force saw little resistance, but it was the first conflict to put the Eagle to the test in aerial combat and a rugged environment. *USAF*

This photograph shows four F-15Cs lined up in standard fingertip-takeoff position preparing for night launch. Two pairs of Eagles patrolled no-fly zones in loose formation. They sometimes tanked twice before heading home. Upon return, the four aircraft approached the base in echelon formation for the high-speed break to landing. *Tyson V. Rininger*

(OAF). It was hoped that F-15Cs relocated to Aviano AB, Italy, flying CAP support over the hostile area, would provide a show of force that would encourage Milosevic to meet NATO requests. Strike assets from the USAF in support of NATO continued to grow as Kosovo remained occupied. This led to NATO implementation of Operation Noble Anvil.

As stated by the U.S. Secretary of Defense in a prepared statement to the Armed Services Committee on April 15, 1999, "Our military objective is to degrade and damage the military and security structure that President Milosevic has used to depopulate and destroy the Albanian majority in Kosovo." Two weeks prior on March 24–26, F-15C pilots from the 493rd Tactical Fighter Squadron shot down four MiG-29s.

On September 11, 2001, Eagles took to the sky to defend the United States on its home soil following terrorist attacks on the World Trade Center and the U.S. Pentagon. As the entire country became a NFZ, F-15s patrolled America's borders while maintaining a security presence over the country's largest and most venerable cities, including Washington, D.C.

Operation Enduring Freedom (OEF) kept Eagles in the air over various parts of the world. Established on September 20, 2001, in response to the September 11 terrorist attacks, OEF originally sought out Osama bin Laden and Taliban forces thought to be behind the attacks. Five ultimatums were made to the Taliban as part of Operation Enduring Freedom—Afghanistan (OEF-A):

1. Deliver to the United States all of the leaders of al Qaeda.
2. Release all imprisoned foreign nationals.
3. Close immediately every terrorist training camp.
4. Hand over every terrorist and their supporters to appropriate authorities.
5. Give the United States full access to terrorist training camps for inspection.

The Taliban quickly rejected these terms, stating there was no evidence bin Laden was behind the terrorist actions. The next day, the United Arab Emirates (UAE) and, soon after, Saudi Arabia rejected the Taliban as being the legal government of Afghanistan. Negotiations continued with the Taliban regarding bin Laden's removal and trial, but without resolve. On October 7, 2001, air strikes

Originally operated by the 53rd Tactical Fighter Squadron based at Bitburg, Germany, this Eagle was one of two flown on a historic sortie, February 6, 1991. Captain Thomas Dietz, flying airframe 79-0078 (pictured above), and Lt. Bob Hehemann in Eagle 84-0019 shot down two aircraft each during Operation Desert Storm. Dietz shot down two MiG-21s while Hehemann downed two Su-25s. The aircraft currently serves with the 58th Fighter Squadron at Eglin Air Force Base, Florida. *Tyson V. Rininger*

utilizing F-15Es, B-52 Stratofortress, B-1B Lancer, and B-2 Spirit bombers ensued on presumed bin Laden hideouts and Taliban training camps. Once again, F-15Cs were called in to fly aerial support protecting the large bombers, intelligence aircraft, and tankers.

Operation Enduring Freedom consisted of multiple operations in locations around the world in an effort to fight terrorism. Besides OEF-A, there were missions in the Philippines (OEF-P) formerly known as Operation Freedom Eagle, the Horn of Africa (OEF-HOA), and the Trans Sahara (OEF-TS). While most of Afghanistan was patrolled by U.S. and coalition air forces, OEF-HOA and OEF-P received support mainly from naval forces. OEF-TS received a small contingency of ground

This in-flight view shows two USAF F-15C Eagles of the 33rd Tactical Fighter Wing, Eglin Air Force Base, Florida, and a Royal Saudi Air Force F-5E Tiger II fighter during an Operation Desert Storm mission. Armed with air-to-air AIM-9 Sidewinder missiles, the F-15 pictured closest is the flagship of the 33rd, Gulf Spirit 85-0118. That honor later transferred to 85-0102 after three enemy aircraft were shot down over two sorties. *USAF*

ANTI-SATELLITE MISSILES (ASATS)

It was thought at one point that nearly three-fourths of all satellites rotating earth were being used for military purposes. By 1971, the Soviet Union was known to have an anti-satellite system in place and the United States had once again, like the MiG-25 surprise, fallen behind. Unlike what the United States would eventually develop, the Soviet Union had a satellite in place that would destroy other satellites.

The USAF saw the F-15 Eagle as a potential platform for what would become an air-launched miniature vehicle (ALMV) with a

multi-stage rocket. Development of the rocket began in 1977 and Vought was awarded the contract in 1979.

The anti-satellite missile or ASAT consisted of three stages. The first stage consisted of an SR75-LP-1 solid-propellant rocket from the AGM-69 SRAM missile and was subcontracted to Boeing for production. The second stage contained the inertial guidance package and a Thiokol FW-4S motor that was built by Vought. The third stage was the most complex due to it containing a liquid helium

Flying over the Vandenberg Air Force Base Satellite Tracking Station, Eagle 76-0086 demonstrates the enormous size of the anti-satellite missile. *USAF*

forces in an effort to keep terrorists away from mainland Europe. These operations and other smaller non-U.S.-involved conflicts all fell under the Global War on Terrorism (GWOT).

The United States, backed by British forces and smaller contingents from Australia, Poland, and Denmark, led the 2003 invasion of Iraq. Iraq's

cooperation with al Qaeda, along with intelligence reports claiming the existence of Weapons of Mass Destruction (WMDs), enforced the reasoning behind the invasion. Furthermore, it was believed that continued terrorist activity was being funded by Iraq and supported by Saddam Hussein. By December 2003, coalition forces captured Hussein and executed

system enabling the infrared sensor to remain cool. This stage, also known as the miniature kill vehicle, housed a guidance computer, roll reference sensor, and solid rocket motors for maneuverability, activated by a hydrazine attitude control system.

The miniature kill vehicle's central computer system weighed a mere 0.8 pounds. The sixty-three maneuver motors measured 0.5 inch each in diameter and managed to squeeze out 10,000 PSI during their 0.1-second burn time.

Weighing in at 2,600 pounds with a length just shy of eighteen feet, only fifteen ASM-135As were built and of those, six were flight-tested. SAC coordinated mission planning for the flight tests at Cheyenne Mountain complex in Colorado. Although the pilot was given an advanced heads-up display with pertinent information not found on standard F-15As, coordinates vectoring the F-15 to the correct location and launch time were still relayed through SAC.

Upon launch, the ASM-135A's first stage fired and propelled the missile to the precise inertial point required for satellite collision. The second stage used the guidance package to keep the third stage on track. This enabled the infrared system to detect the target despite the satellite being hundreds of miles away. The MKV spun at a rate of thirty-three revolutions per second in order to keep track of altitude while the infrared system continued to track its target and relay that information to the guidance system. Upon command of the central computer, the MKV's solid rocket motors fired to accomplish its final precision maneuver. The ASAT contained no warhead, as the kinetic energy alone would decimate the target. Closing velocity of the satellite and missile were expected to approach 15,000 to 25,000 miles per hour, ensuring total destruction.

A live fire was conducted on September 13, 1985, with Major Doug Pearson flying airframe 76-0084. The target, considered beyond its service life, was a 1,874-pound, 6.8-foot diameter P78-1 satellite orbiting about 290 miles above the earth's surface. The missile hit within six inches of the target area. The USAF described the test as flawless.

Because continued testing would potentially violate treaties regarding military use of space, this was the only launch of its kind.

The only aircraft to rightfully claim a satellite kill, Eagle 76-0084 fires a live ASM-135A over the Pacific Ocean on September 13, 1985. Hitting the satellite within six inches of the targeted area, the exercise was deemed flawless, though the program was eventually cancelled. *USAF*

him after a trial in December 2006. Just like OEF, F-15s maintained a presence in the skies while F-15Es continued to launch attacks against remaining Iraqi military hardware, al Qaeda hideouts, and any other potential threat.

F-15C Eagles and F-15E Strike Eagles maintained air and ground supremacy. They restored democracy to Afghanistan and Iraq, proved their worth, and earned a place in the history books as the most successful modern day jet fighter ever built. As of 2008, F-15s of all models and operating forces have shot down a total of 104 aircraft with zero losses.

RIGHT The 1992 UN resolution Operation Deny Flight protected UN forces while assisting humanitarian efforts in Bosnia and Herzegovina. Following attacks by Serbia and Montenegro, the UN ordered reinforcements in the form of Operation Deliberate Force. F-15s played the all-important role of escort and interdiction that kept the larger, unarmed aircraft such as tankers and AWACS safe from attack.

BELOW Airman First Class Abram Groves, crew chief of the 379th Expeditionary Air Maintenance Squadron, uses the solvent Penair on the intake of an F-15C during Operation Iraqi Freedom. Crews usually cleaned intakes every other week because of the airborne dust and sand prevalent in the area. *USAF*

LEFT A view from a KC-135R Stratotanker from the 909th Air Refueling Squadron as it refuels an F-15C Eagle from the 67th Fighter Squadron while on a mission two hundred nautical miles east of Okinawa. Both units are from the 18th Wing, Kadena Air Base, Japan. The 67th served in both Operation Iraqi Freedom and Operation Southern Watch. *USAF*

BELOW Airmen assigned to the 485th Expeditionary Aircraft Maintenance Squadron perform scheduled maintenance on an F-15C. They are at a forward-deployed location in Southwest Asia during Operation Iraqi Freedom. The Eagle's incredible performance throughout the war was due in large part to the men and women on the ground. *USAF*

An F-15E from the 90th Fighter Squadron based in Elmendorf, Alaska, blasts off from Nellis Air Force Base, Nevada, putting the twin PW-220s in full afterburner. Sixty other aircraft participated in the realistic Red Flag exercise. Strike Eagle 87-0204 currently serves with the 366 Fighter Wing, 389th Fighter Squadron, in Mountain Home Air Force Base, Idaho. *Tyson V. Rininger*

CHAPTER FOUR

F-15E STRIKE EAGLE

THROUGHOUT THE F-15S DEVELOPMENT, battles wore on between the air superiority purists and those wanting a multi-role aircraft. The motto, "Not a pound for air-to-ground," echoed through the halls of the developers in an attempt to save weight and increase thrust-to-weight ratios, fuel efficiency, aerial combat effectiveness, and many other aspects that eventually made the Eagle so successful.

McAir engineers and Eagle pilots (known as "drivers" among the pilots themselves) saw the potential opportunities the F-15 platform could provide should air-to-ground technology and tactics

Despite the winning design of the variable-geometry airframe, the swept-wing aircraft's failures put the Strike Eagle in a promising position for success. As the TFX program, later known as the F-111, gained political support and entered production, shortcomings continuously marred its development and paved the way for the introduction of the Strike Eagle. *USAF*

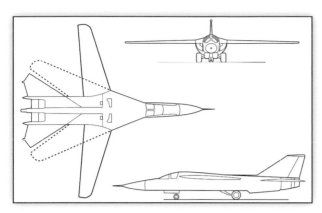

Testing of NASA's X-5, the first variable-geometry aircraft, revealed problems with the F-111. Close hinge-points caused stress on the swing mechanism, and the aircraft was too long for an aircraft carrier's elevator system. Even though the swing-wing was designed to assist the aircraft at low speeds for a carrier landing, the entire aircraft weighed far too much for practical USN applications. *USAF*

be employed. With the need for a replacement of the current fighter-designated bomber, the F-111, McDonnell Douglas embarked to create an entirely new aircraft utilizing the existing platform.

The F-111 Aardvark was a result of a USN request for a low-altitude strike fighter. Initial requests were based on the design of the British NA-39 with the addition of variable sweep-wing technology. To maximize the aircraft's capabilities, the DoD devised the Tactical Fighter Experimental (TFX) program to create a supersonic multi-role fighter-bomber for both the USAF and USN. This new fighter was intended to replace the McDonnell Douglas F-4 Phantom II and carrier-based Vought F-8 Crusader as well as the extremely fast Lockheed F-105 Starfighter.

The idea was to devise an aircraft that could reach a high-altitude speed of Mach 2.5, carry nuclear weapons internally, fly transatlantic routes nonstop even without

Ultimately, the F-111 served the USAF and the Royal Australian Air Force with a production total of about 600 aircraft instead of the originally proposed 1,700 airframes. Grumman studied the F-111 and created the venerable F-14 Tomcat for the USN. It also had a swing-wing but with sturdier and further separated hinge-points. Upon retirement of the EF-111A Raven electronic-warfare platform, Grumman again stepped up and provided the USAF with the EA-6B Prowler. *USAF*

McDonnell Douglas knew the modified F-15's potential as a multi-role fighter. Here an artist's concept of F-15E Strike Eagle shows the assortment of bombs and air-to-air missiles the aircraft could bring to combat. *USAF*

refueling, and operate from rough airfields. In 1961, Secretary of Defense Robert McNamara requested in an industry-wide RFP the development of a single, multi-purpose aircraft suitable for both the USN and USAF. Although the USN and USAF were both trying to accommodate the DoD by devising a single fighter suitable for both services, neither branch could agree on a suitable airframe. McNamara was forced to step in and devise the RFP.

Meanwhile, NASA and the Langley Research Center were working on developing swept-wing technology. It seemed to be the perfect answer for a multi-service aircraft. A swept-wing craft would

be able to fly slow enough and maintain control for carrier-based operations as well as high-altitude, high-speed intercept and bombing missions.

Both Boeing and General Dynamics were offered continued RFPs but were turned down when their designs failed to meet the requirements. Boeing presented a final design that promised to meet the RFP requirements and even exceed them with a lower-than-estimated cost per aircraft. All of the senior military advisors were pleased with the submission, and Boeing received the contract. Political scientist Robert Art, writing in 1968, noted, "In the fourth evaluation there was thus unanimity—absolutely

Among a gathering of F-15Es and a lone F-16C from Mountain Home Air Force Base, a USN EA-6B Prowler (foreground) assists with radar jamming and electronic countermeasures during an exercise. Originally, the EF-111B Raven performed these duties. However it was more economical to retire the Raven and incorporate the assistance of the USN for various electronic warfare tasks. *USAF*

no dissent—up through the entire military chain of command, in recommending the Boeing Company." McNamara again stepped in and overruled Boeing's victory regarding the first four initial steps of production. Instead, he gave General Dynamics and Grumman the opportunity to build the TFX on November 21, 1962.

Questions and concerns regarding the TFX surfaced before production began. Senator John Little McClellan of Arkansas held hearings regarding the companies awarded the TFX program brought up by Senator Henry M. Jackson of Washington. Despite being called to testify to the committee regarding McNamara's sole decision to counter all other military

opinions, Jackson signed the authorization to continue development of the aircraft on the day of his hearing.

Despite the political turmoil, the first USAF F-111A flew in December 1964, and the USN variant, the F-111B, took to the skies in May 1965. Use of the VG swept-wing system proved a resounding success though the aircraft still seemed underpowered. Aerodynamic efficiency and induced drag were of great concern to the USN. As the Assistant Secretary of the Air Force was being informed of the condition, Langley engineers were working with wind tunnel models to arrive at a solution.

Engineers determined the wing pivot location was the main cause of induced drag and should

Technician Sue Gerdts mounts an F-15E Strike Eagle model for simulation of refueling operations. The model provides visual simulation of a receiver aircraft for boom operator training. The KC-10 Extender Simulator Center is at March Air Force Reserve Base near Riverside, California. *USAF*

be moved outward. Unfortunately, this advice was ignored on the F-111 design, seriously jeopardizing the F-111B's potential USN success. Grumman continued to look into ways of solving the problem. Eventually, they moved the pivot points outward on the F-14 Tomcat (the USN's impending answer to the failed F-111B).

Additional problems with the F-111B continued to plague the TFX program. The Navy's use of the aircraft was becoming doubtful. Engine failures and efficiency anomalies plagued the project as low altitude, high-speed flights resulted in disappointing range figures. The program was dropped completely when the aircraft was deemed too heavy for carrier-based

operations, but the airframe was simply too long to fit on the carrier's elevator.

The USAF continued utilizing the F-111A, incorporating various airframe, engine, and avionics modifications. The D model featured revised intakes that prevented ingestion of turbulent surface airflow known to occasionally stall out the original TF-30 engines. Additionally, more powerful TF30-P-3 engines were also installed. The E model took advantage of the new upgrades of the D but due to teething problems, reverted back to the A model avionics package. The F-111F was effectively a D model with the improved Mark IIB avionics package. The G variant underwent major improvements

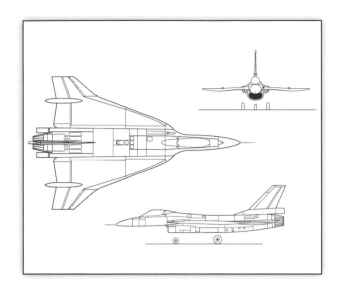

LEFT General Dynamics attempted to rectify the shortcomings of its F-111 by introducing the highly modified F-16E, better known as the F-16XL. The capacity for internal fuel was increased over the base F-16 by incorporating a blended body-and-wing design. This also expanded the overall lift from the larger wing area. This created more room for hardpoints, enabling a greater weapons capacity. *USAF*

BELOW This McDonnell Douglas's prototype, airframe 71-0291, is lacking the CFTs and is adorned in green camouflage. It originally served as TF-2, the second two-seat F-15B, constructed for stability, control, and performance tests. It later sported a custom paint scheme to celebrate the American Bicentennial. The aircraft is currently a trainer for airframe battle damage repair (ABDR) at Robins Air Force Base, Georgia. *USAF*

upgrading to a digital computer system, Doppler navigation, and terrain-following radar.

The aircraft was never able to recover from the political issues caused by McNamara. Furthermore, the USN's exclusion didn't help justify the originally estimated 1,700 F-111s. In all, approximately six hundred aircraft of all variations were built. The the final version was the EF-111A Raven. Intended to replace the aging Douglas EB-66, the Raven was modified by Grumman to create an electronic warfare-electronic countermeasure (ECM) airframe.

Two years after the retirement of frontline F-111s, the EF-111A was also retired in May 1998. As of 2008, the USN's Grumman EA-6B Prowler was still assisting the USAF in ECM operations.

The USAF sought to replace the F-111 in March 1981, with the announcement of the enhanced tactical fighter program. Similar to the original requirements of the Aardvark, the enhanced tactical fighter was to have supersonic, deep interdiction mission capability with nuclear deployment. In addition, the aircraft needed to be self-sustaining and able to complete a

An F-15E from the 46th Test Wing, 40th Flight Test Squadron, based at Eglin Air Force Base, Florida, is loaded with weapons to test flight characteristics and payload handling. Cameras mounted in various positions throughout the airframe catch any type of adverse weapons movement due to vortices or wake turbulence. *USAF*

Major Allan Reed of the 6510th Test Wing was the first test pilot to fly the F-15E Strike Eagle through the skies over the California desert. *USAF*

Colonel J. O. McFalls III, 4th Tactical Fighter Wing, climbs out of the cockpit of the "Spirit of Goldsboro" at the end of a four-hour flight from Luke Air Force Base, Arizona. With McFalls's arrival at Seymour-Johnson Air Force Base, the 4th Tactical Fighter Wing became the first operational USAF unit to receive the potent F-15E. *USAF*

mission without the use of additional escort fighter aircraft including ECM support.

McDonnell Douglas and General Dynamics each submitted designs for the successor of the F-111. General Dynamics learned from experience the deficiencies of the F-111 and had just produced the extremely successful F-16A Fighting Falcon. McDonnell Douglas, meanwhile, was basking in the success of the F-15 program, supplying airframes at a rate of nine per month along with providing Eagles to other allied nations.

Hoping to capitalize on the F-16's success as a fighter, General Dynamics introduced the F-16E, also known as the F-16XL. The F-16XL had a modified delta wing running the entire length of the airframe. With the fuselage lengthened, the delta wing took the place of the supersonic stabilators and added hardpoint length for additional payload.

McDonnell Douglas had a slight advantage over General Dynamics as the F-15 airframe had been developed with multi-role capability in mind all along. To keep the investors happy, "not a pound for air-to-ground" was enforced though continued pressure from multi-role insistent parties at TAC during development had trickled through in the eventual design.

Four months before the USAF submitted the RFP, McDonnell Douglas offered a proposal for a Strike Eagle variant with ground-attack capability. The proposal suggested fitting existing F-15 airframes with improved avionics that would provide the Eagles with the ability to assume multi-role capability. The program consisted of

Mayor Hal K. Plonk of Goldsboro, North Carolina, presents ceremonial keys to Col. James E. Little (left), director of operations for the 4th Tactical Fighter Wing, and Col. Gary Herman (center), deputy commander for maintenance. The keys commemorate the arrival of the wing's first F-15E Strike Eagle, "Spirit of Goldsboro." *USAF*

The pilot and weapons system officer (WSO) see this type of view when using the low-altitude navigation and targeting infrared for night (LANTIRN) system. A projected infrared image on the heads up display (HUD) enables low-terrain, adverse weather, nighttime flight, and precision weapons deployment. *USAF*

retrofitting 144 TAC Eagles, 206 F-15A and B models, along with 304 C and D models currently serving with other tactical forces.

Although the contract for the multi-role fighter had not yet been awarded, McDonnell Douglas was still revising the F-15A-D models. From August 1982, through September 1983, F-15C test aircraft were performing air-to-ground evaluations at Edwards Air Force Base as well as testing the newly designed, removable conformal fuel tanks.

On February 24, 1984, McDonnell Douglas won the contract for continued development and production of the F-15E Strike Eagle. Costing an estimated $1.5 billion, the USAF planned to take delivery of 393 two-seat F-15Es. McAir was asked to improve further the air-to-ground capabilities of the aircraft being tested thus far. On April 27, 1984, HQAF issued the directive required to begin development of the new aircraft.

On March 31, 1987, the first officially completed F-15E took to the skies. A year later, in April 1988, the 405th Tactical Training Wing at Luke Air Force Base received the first Strike Eagle and began the training process. By September 30, 1989, IOC was achieved through the 336th Tactical Fighter Squadron, 4th Tactical Fighter Wing at Seymour-Johnson Air Force Base, North Carolina, headquarters for TAC. Unfortunately, difficulty in obtaining parts forced the F-15E to achieve only limited operational capability until the following year.

The Strike Eagle was designed as a two-place fighter-bomber incorporating the use of a weapons system officer (WSO), or "wizzo." With a maximum take-off weight of 81,000 pounds, the F-15E could carry

4TH FIGHTER WING HISTORY

Spanning more than five decades and five wars, the 4th Fighter Wing is one of the most distinguished fighter units in the world. In addition, it has the distinction of being one of only two Air Force units that can trace its history to another country.

Before the United States's entry into World War II, American volunteers were already serving as combat veterans in Royal Air Force Eagle Squadrons (71st, 121st, and 133rd). When the United States entered the war, these units, and the American pilots in them, were transferred to the U.S. Army Air Forces 8th Air Force, forming the 4th Fighter Group on September 12, 1942.

The 4th Fighter Group (with squadrons now designated the 334th, 335th, and 336th) was a record setter throughout the air war over Europe, justly earning the motto, "Fourth But First."

It was the first fighter group to use belly tanks, the first to penetrate Germany, the first to accompany bombers to Berlin, the first to accomplish the England-to-Russia shuttle and the first to down jet fighters. The group was credited with the destruction of 1,016 enemy aircraft, more than any other 8th Air Force unit, and produced thirty-eight aces.

The 4th Fighter Group was inactivated at Camp Kilmer, New Jersey, November 10, 1945. It was reactivated at Selfridge Field,

Michigan, September 9, 1946, as the United States began to rearm due to Cold War pressures.

Following a period of training with F-80 Shooting Star aircraft, the 4th Fighter Group transitioned to F-86 Sabre jets in March 1949, just in time for advanced training and entry into the Korean War.

In December 1950, the group (now designated the 4th Fighter-Interceptor Group) was the first unit to commit F-86 Sabre jets to the Korean War. Lieutenant Colonel Bruce H. Hinton shot down a MiG-15 on December 17, during the first Sabre mission of the war. Four days later, Lt. Col. John C. Meyer, a World War II ace, led elements of the group into the first major all-jet fighter battle in history. They downed six MiG-15s without sustaining any losses. Fourth airmen destroyed 502 enemy aircraft (54 percent of the total), becoming the top fighter unit of the Korean War. Twenty-four pilots achieved ace status.

Now associated with the 4th Fighter-Interceptor Wing, the group moved to Japan following the Korean armistice in 1953. They continued training and tours to Korea. The unit moved to Seymour Johnson Air Force Base, North Carolina, December 8, 1957. There they picked up a fourth tactical fighter squadron and were redesignated as the 4th Tactical Fighter Wing in July 1958. The

This commemorative photograph was taken during the conversion process. A 335th Tactical Fighter Squadron F-4E Phantom II flies alongside a 335th Tactical Fighter Squadron F-15E Eagle over the North Carolina coastline. *USAF*

Departing Nellis Air Force Base, an F-15E from Seymour Johnson is just shy of coming clean with gear doors closing. The Strike Eagle pictured is in the two-bag configuration, a reference to the two large fuel tanks slung underneath the wings. The F-15E also carries the newer AIM-9X Sidewinder missile. *Tyson V. Rininger*

333rd "Lancers" remained with the 4th Wing until reassignment to Pacific Air Forces December 4, 1965.

Aircrews of the 4th flew F-100 Super Sabre aircraft at the new location. Within two years, the wing became the first Air Force unit to convert to F-105 Thunderchief aircraft. During the transitioning phase, a new world speed record was set for the 100-kilometer closed course at Edwards Air Force Base, California. Brigadier General Joseph H. Moore, 4th wing commander, established the new record of 1,163.35 miles per hour.

Some of the more significant events of the 1960s included: the deployment of the three tactical fighter squadrons to McCoy Air Force Base, Florida, during the Cuban missile crisis in October 1962; rotational tours to Southeast Asia in 1965; and transition to F-4D Phantom II aircraft beginning in early 1967. The readiness posture of the wing was given a true test in early 1968. The North Koreans seized the *Pueblo*, an American intelligence-gathering ship, just off the coast of North Korea. Elements of the 4th moved to Korea within seventy-two hours.

The 4th Fighter Wing continued to sustain a highly visible mobility posture with development of the first operationally ready, bare-base squadron in 1970, followed by multiple deployments to Southeast Asia beginning in April 1972. Operating from Ubon Royal Thai Air Base, Thailand, as the first F-4 wing to augment elements of Pacific Air Forces, aircrews of the 4th flew more than 8,000 combat missions, many into the very heart of North Vietnam.

Following on the heels of Constant Guard operations in Southeast Asia, the Fourth executed Peace Echo operations in October 1973, an almost instantaneous response to critical events in the Middle East, which helped restore a balance of power in that troubled part of the world.

In 1974, the wing mission reverted back to training with increased emphasis on short-term European contingency support. Elements of the wing deployed to Norway in June 1974. Two short-term deployments to Spangdahlem Air Base, Germany, were conducted in July and September 1975. The highlight of 1976 came in November when the wing took first place in the William Tell worldwide weapons competition at Tyndall Air Force Base, Florida, becoming the first F-4 unit to win the Air Defense Command-sponsored event. The wing executed short-term deployments to Korea and Japan during 1977, and assumed a dual-based mission (with Ramstein AB, Germany) in October of that year. The overall mission commitment was restructured to reflect worldwide contingency emphasis in October 1986.

Beginning in late 1980, the wing began converting to ARN-101-equipped aircraft to enhance bombing and navigation capabilities. In September 1981 and in October 1983, the wing won the prestigious Gunsmoke meet in the F-4 ARN-101 category. The meet was held at Nellis Air Force Base, Nevada, where in January 1985, the "Fourth But First" became the first operational unit to conduct live drops of the GBU-15.

With assignment of a fourth tactical fighter squadron (the 337th "Falcons") on April 1, 1982, the 4th was recognized as one of the Air Force's largest operational tactical fighter units. The 337th was inactivated July 1, 1985.

In 1988, the 4th began transitioning to the F-15E Strike Eagle, the Air Force's newest and most advanced tactical fighter aircraft. The first F-15E arrived December 29, 1988, and the 336th Tactical Fighter Squadron became the first operational F-15E squadron in the USAF October 1, 1989. The transition from the F-4E to the F-15E was completed July 1, 1991, making the 4th Fighter Wing the first operational F-15E wing.

At the height of conversion training, the 4th was one of the first units tasked to react to Iraq's invasion of Kuwait August 2, 1990. Two F-15E tactical fighter squadrons were deployed to Southwest Asia in August and December of that year. The unit earned another first by spearheading nighttime strikes against Iraqi forces January 16, 1991, helping bring the Persian Gulf War to a successful conclusion February 28.

On April 22, 1991, the 4th became the Air Force's first composite wing. The 4th Tactical Fighter Wing was redesignated the 4th Wing and incorporated under it all the people, KC-10 aircraft, and assets of the 68th Air Refueling Wing, a Strategic Air Command unit.

The 4th began a force structure change in 1994. The KC-10s were reassigned to Air Mobility Command bases in 1994 and 1995, and the F-15E formal training unit moved to Seymour Johnson in 1994 and 1995. The 333rd Fighter Squadron returned to Seymour Johnson to accommodate the training mission. Following the departure of KC-10s, the 4th Wing was redesignated the 4th Fighter Wing on December 1, 1995. To accommodate the need to train more F-15E aircrews, the 334th Fighter Squadron became a training squadron on January 1, 1996.

Fewer resources and the need to use all USAF assets to meet increased operational commitments called for yet another reorganization. The expeditionary aerospace force concept is the Air Force vision to organize, train, equip, deploy, and sustain itself in the twenty-first-century global security environment. Under the concept, the 4th Fighter Wing is one of two on-call rapid response

aerospace expeditionary wings. The 4th was the first to assume this on-call mission on October 1, 1999.

On June 20, 2000, the 23rd Fighter Group became a part of the 4th Fighter Wing, during a reassignment ceremony at Pope Air Force Base, North Carolina, and continues to operate from Fayetteville, North Carolina. The group flies and maintains A-10A Thunderbolt II aircraft. Their primary mission is forward air control, close-air support, interdiction, and combat search and rescue operations. The ceremony brought together two organizations whose histories predate the United States involvement in World War II, when both units served as American volunteer groups.

In January 2001, the 4th Fighter Wing became the proud recipient of the Commander-In-Chief's Installation Excellence Award. The 4th received a one million dollar prize for quality of life and job enhancement. The honor proves the hard work and dedication of all members of the 4th as the "best base in the Air Force."

In October 2001, in response to the September 11 terrorist attacks on the United States, the 4th Fighter Wing began flying Operation Noble Eagle sorties, the first of its kind for the wing, providing coastal protection for Homeland Defense.

In January 2002, the 4th Fighter Wing arrived in Kuwait in support of Operations Southern Watch and Enduring Freedom, flying missions over Iraq and Afghanistan. On March 1, 2002, Operation Anaconda was launched, and the wing's mission was to provide close air support into Afghanistan. Operation Anaconda ended March 21, 2002, with the 4th Fighter Wing's greatest highlight being their performance at Roberts Ridge. Members of the 335th Fighter Squadron successfully suppressed enemy fire from al-Qaida troops, as Army and Air Force personnel retrieved stranded and fallen comrades.

In March 2002, A-10s assigned to the 23rd Fighter Group from Pope Air Force Base, North Carolina, arrived in Jacobabad, Pakistan, and later became the first fixed-wing aircraft to enter Afghanistan to fight the war on terrorism.

On September 1, 2002, the 4th transitioned into its final on-call AEW. Though the 4th Fighter Wing will continue as a lead wing when deployed, it will now assimilate into the more predictable ninety-day ten AEF schedule, as opposed to waiting for the call from higher headquarter.

In January and February 2003, in response to the threat of Iraq's ability to produce weapons of mass destruction (WMD) and their elusiveness with United Nation weapon inspectors, the 4th Fighter Wing joined other operational units in Southeast Asia. Two F-15E fighter squadrons were deployed to Southwest Asia in support of Operation Southern Watch and later for Operation Iraqi Freedom. On April 18, 2003, members of the 4th Fighter Wing returned heroically to Seymour Johnson Air Force Base after contributing to the resounding U.S.-led coalition victory over Iraq.

an external payload of up to 24,500 pounds, consisting of missiles, bombs, fuel tanks, and electronics pods. The F-15E was designed to be self-sufficient, fighting its way to the target, completing the target object, and fighting its way back without the assistance of outside forces or escort aircraft. To achieve that goal, the aircraft is equipped to fly in any kind of weather, day or night, in either air-to-air or air-to-ground roles.

Up front, the pilot has the option of viewing all pertinent flight information via the HUD. He can also glance at the small forward-looking infrared monitor that presents a daytime view of the surrounding terrain regardless of weather or nightfall.

In back, the WSO's office is like no other fighter-bomber previously developed. The instrument panel is equipped with four image monitors capable of displaying visual data from the onboard radar system, infrared sensors, weapons status, potential threats, and much more. The WSO also has the ability to navigate through scrolling maps or move information from one display to another through the use of two hand controls.

Assisting the crew is the low-altitude navigation and targeting infrared for night (LANTIRN) system that allows for precise guided munitions delivery. Additionally, the F-15E is equipped with an advanced avionics system enabling the crew to fly in lower altitudes (known in the USAF as "map of the earth"), in adverse weather, day or night. This is done via inertial navigation system (INS) utilizing a laser gyro that continuously transmits the aircraft's location to the central computer system

Airmen assigned to the 4th Equipment Maintenance Squadron, Seymour Johnson Air Force Base, remove a CFT from an F-15E on the flight line at Nellis Air Force Base, during exercise Combat Hammer. Unlike the F-15Cs, the Strike Eagles are rarely seen without CFTs due to their additional drag and subsequent need for more fuel. *USAF*

Jet engine test cell technicians Staff Sgt. Fernando Suarez, Mr. Jessie Melton, and Staff Sgt. Adam Nichols, assigned to the 57th Component Maintenance Squadron, perform maintenance on a P&W F-100-PW-220 F-15E engine inside the test cell hush house at Nellis Air Force Base. The revised engine replaced the problematic PW-100 and came as a dream to many Strike Eagle pilots. *USAF*

and relays the information through preprogrammed mission maps. In conjunction with the LANTIRN system, the pilot has the choice of following cues provided through the HUD to ease the strain of low-level flight or choosing the autopilot mode whereby the aircraft will assume the hands-off terrain-following capability.

In the nose of the Strike Eagle lies the APG-70 radar system. More advanced than the F-15Cs APG-63, the APG-70 has the ability to detect objects further than one hundred miles away and provide their speed, altitude, exact distance, and other information. Crisp images providing extreme target detail are provided through synthetic aperture radar technology. Similar to the APG-63, synthetic aperture radar uses Doppler shift technology and simply enhances the radar return for crisp, sharp images.

To pilots, utilizing all of the Strike Eagle's advanced features seemed to be a daunting task. The addition of a WSO was one way of sharing the workload, HOTAS was the other. Just as on the F-15A-C models, HOTAS enabled the pilot and WSO (in the case of the F-15E) to control the cockpit's seven different monitors without taking their hands off the throttle or stick. To rotate a screen from one map to another, a button was simply pressed on the throttle. This enabled the crew to better concentrate on flying the aircraft rather than becoming overtasked with the workings of the cockpit.

Originally tested on the F-15C, the low-drag CFT normally found on the F-15E have a capacity of 750 extra gallons of fuel each. Not only do the CFTs provide greater fuel capacity with minimum drag, they also contain six additional short pylons each for maximizing kills per sortie. Unlike the pylon-

More than fifty F-15E Strike Eagles assigned to the 4th Fighter Wing, Seymour Johnson Air Force Base, are lined up on the runway with B-52H Stratofortress aircraft. This rare grouping of aircraft at Barksdale Air Force Base, Louisiana, was an effort to avoid hurricane Bertha. *USAF*

mounted fuel tanks typically seen on the F-15A-C models, the CFTs are unable to be jettisoned, and while they do produce some drag when empty, CFTs are still more aerodynamic than conventional external teardrop tanks. As with the air superiority version of the F-15, the USAF deemed the additional drag too inefficient, and therefore CFTs are rarely carried though the need for an extended range to complete a multi-role mission suited the F-15E perfectly

Like the F-15A-C, the Strike Eagle utilizes the CAS to provide excellent handling abilities at all speeds within the aircraft's flight envelope. Two, separate hydromechanical systems provide inputs to the three primary flight controls enabling pitch, yaw, and roll. Should either system fail, the redundant controls will enable the crew to return safely home.

Using CAS is somewhat straightforward. However, it is mechanically complex. While pitch movements require the stabilators to move in a conventional manner, roll inputs require the stabilators to move in opposite directions. This becomes more difficult to manage as aircraft speeds increase. The Control

A Strike Eagle from the 335th Fighter Squadron based at Seymour Johnson Air Force Base, returns from a Red Flag mission. While the F-15C Eagles fly intercept and aerial supremacy missions, the F-15E Strike Eagles engage ground targets at certain locations throughout the vast Nellis Range Complex northeast of Las Vegas, Nevada. *Tyson V. Rininger*

Aerial of an F-15E Strike Eagle, 335th Fighter Squadron, 4th Fighter Wing, deployed from Seymour Johnson Air Force Base over Iraq. The Strike Eagle is armed with AIM-120A AMRAAM, AIM-9M Sidewinder missiles, GBU-12 500–pound bombs, and equipped with an AN/AAQ-28 (V) LITENING AT targeting pod. *USAF*

Augmentation System modifies pilot inputs to keep the aircraft stable regardless of airspeed.

Also assisting the pilot is the aileron-rudder interconnect, which manually joins the rudders and ailerons to the pilot's control stick. In conventional flight, a coordinated turn requires a small degree of rudder input. The aileron-rudder interconnect system automatically inputs a small amount of rudder based on the desired turn radius. At supersonic speed, the physics of flight changes dramatically and rudder inputs are rarely, if ever, used. Therefore, at speeds above Mach 1, the aileron-rudder interconnect system is automatically disengaged.

Another major improvement was to the Strike Eagle's powerplant. Keeping with the P&W design, McDonnell Douglas chose to use the more advanced F100-PW-220 engines with increased performance using a digital electronic engine control system. Producing just over 25,000 pounds of thrust each, the digital system enables the pilot quicker engine response time, which in turn provides better acceleration and improved maneuvering.

Less than a year after receiving IOC, the F-15E was called to duty to participate in Operation Desert Shield and later Desert Storm in August 1990, when Iraq invaded Kuwait. First to fly were the 335th Tactical Fighter Squadron Chiefs and the 336th Tactical Fighter Squadron Rocketeers. A week following the invasion, the two squadrons headed to Seeb Air Base in Oman where they provided defensive measures since only a limited amount of weaponry was qualified to be carried by the aircraft at the time. Weapons tested and approved for combat were limited to the Mk82 and Mk84, though soft cluster bombs were in the process of being tested in the United States and were approved only on certain hardpoint stations. By December of that year, the two squadrons were relocated to Al Kharj Air Base in Saudi Arabia in order to get them closer to the Iraqi border.

Iraq No-Fly Zone

TURKEY

Irbil

North No-Fly Zone

36°

SYRIA

IRAQ

IRAN

Baghdad
★

South No-Fly Zone

33°

SAUDI ARABIA

KUWAIT

AFNS

The cease-fire agreement ending the Gulf War in 1991, created a no-fly zone in Iraq. It supported humanitarian action to the Kurds north of the thirty-sixth parallel by preventing Iraqi military operations in this area. The southern no-fly zone, created in 1992, was extended to the thirty-third parallel in 1996 to protect the Shi'ite Muslims in the southern areas from Iraqi fighter aircraft. *USAF*

Two weeks into the new year, F-15Es were called upon to destroy threatening surface-to-surface missile systems (SCUD) sites located in western Iraq. A flight of twenty-four F-15Es swarmed the area and took out five SCUD sites. A second flight of twenty-one F-15Es followed using the darkness of night to continue attacks. Despite AWACS tracking SCUD launches, finding the mobile launchers proved to be difficult. Routine F-15E bombing runs over random locations were thought to prevent the establishment of SCUD launch points in certain areas.

Unlike random blind bombing runs such as those tasked with by the Century Series fighters in Vietnam, the role of the F-15E was taken to a more personal level. While various units worked at removing ground threats, tanks, and supposed bunkers, some Strike

Eagles assumed the responsibility of hunting down Saddam Hussein by destroying potential hideouts.

Strike Eagles and A-10 Warthogs had pounded the ground for forty-two days when on March 1, 1991, a ceasefire came in to effect. Immediately, northern and southern no-fly zones were designated. Once established, F-15 Eagles and Strike Eagles, along with a consortium of allied aircraft, cruised the skies patrolling the borders.

For the most part, Iraq heeded the no-fly zones and did well by not testing the patrolling forces. Soon after, ONW and OSW were established. Upon acceptance of ONW, Turkey offered U.S. forces the option of basing aircraft out of Incirlik Air Base. The Black Panthers of the 494th Fighter Squadron were the first to be deployed there in 1993.

The same year, the UN Security Council chose to ban all fixed and rotor wing aircraft over Bosnia-Herzegovina due to the worsening situation in the Balkans. Operation Deny Flight was enforced by F-15Es from the 494th Fighter Squadron and the 492nd Fighter Squadron deployed to Aviano Air Base in Italy. Eight F-15Es were called on by NATO later that year to strike the Ubdina Airfield in Croatia as hostilities with Serbian forces worsened. Tallying more than 2,500 sorties since the inception of Deny Flight, the 492nd and 494th Fighter Squadrons were soon joined by the 90th Fighter Squadron to relieve much of the load. The 492nd logged nearly 2,000 of the 2,500 sorties.

As ONW continued, Operation Desert Fox was conducted in December 1998. This was in response to Iraq's becoming more hostile and less cooperative with the United Nations Special Commission (UNSCOM) inspections. On December 28, three F-15Es dropped two GBU-12s to destroy an SA-3 GOA Soviet-designed SAM site. There was no doubt: the F-15Es were the most highly tasked fighter in the USAF arsenal.

Captain Brian Udell, an F-15E pilot with the 366th Wing, carries a horse saddle to symbolize his being back in the saddle as he returns to the cockpit of the waiting F-15. Udell survived one of the fastest ejections ever recorded on April 18, 1995. Following an uncontrolled dive, Udell and his WSO ejected the aircraft. Udell sustained 780 mile-per-hour winds with only 3,000 feet to spare. The WSO did not survive, and Udell suffered life-threatening injuries, but recovered after ten months of physical therapy. *USAF*

Two F-15E Strike Eagles from the 492nd Fighter Squadron based at Royal Air Force, Lakenheath, England, fly over Iraqi skies. They tuck in close while carrying Paveway Laser Guided Bombs and AIM-120 AMRAAM Slammers during an Operation Iraqi Freedom mission. *USAF*

A clean F-15E from the 334th Fighter Squadron based at Seymour Johnson Air Force Base banks tightly around a smoke-filled sky. The tightly closed exhaust nozzles indicate full afterburner has been selected. When the aircraft reaches supersonic speeds, the nozzles will open. The digital electronic engine control system in the new PW-220 engines helps pilots engage and disengage the aircraft's thrust more quickly and confidently. *Tyson V. Rininger*

Unrest in Kosovo formed the basis for Operation Allied Force in March 1999 when the Serbian government rejected NATO's demand to cease displacement of Kosovars. Once again it was the 492nd and the 494th that were first tasked with the removal of SAM sites, early warning radar stations, and anti-aircraft batteries. They were also some of the first units to conduct close air support missions requiring a variety of weapons including air-to-air and air-to-ground. This allowed them finally to exercise the full potential of the F-15E, enabling it to perform combat air patrols and drop bombs on target prior to their returning back to base.

A month after the devastating attacks of September 11, the Bold Tigers of the 391st Tactical Fighter Squadron, deployed to Ahmed Al Jaber Air Base in Kuwait originally to support OSW. Upon arrival, they found themselves enforcing Operation Enduring Freedom with attacks on Taliban supply depots, strategic buildings, al Qaeda training camps, and even caves thought to be key hideouts for the world's most wanted terrorists. Once most targets had been eliminated, the F-15E was called upon to support American and allied ground forces.

Strike Eagles continued to play a major role in destroying key points in the Taliban resistance. In an effort to flush Taliban and al Qaeda members from hillside caves, the BLU-118/B was used for the first time in combat by an F-15E from the 391st.

Once again, defiance against UNSCOM and intelligence reports suggested the possibility that Iraq

"487" FROM SEYMOUR, MORE THAN JUST PAINT

by James D'Angina, 455th Air Expeditionary Wing History

Bagram Air Field, Afghanistan—Airmen from the 335th Expeditionary Fighter Squadron here are making history daily, as the "Chiefs" from Seymour Johnson Air Force Base, N.C., take the fight to the Anti-Afghanistan Forces in combat operations throughout Afghanistan.

But one of the squadron's aircraft, F-15E Strike Eagle #89-0487, or "487" for short, carries with it a unique distinction in air combat history—it is the only F-15E in the Air Force inventory to be credited with an air-to-air kill.

The historic aircraft deployed in 1991 for Operation Desert Shield/Storm, and has seen multiple deployments in Afghanistan and Iraq supporting Operations Enduring and Iraqi Freedom.

The aircraft, delivered to the 4th Fighter Wing at Seymour Johnson in 1989, was assigned to the 335th Fighter Squadron, a unit with a long and decorated history—over 370 air-to-air kills to its credit.

One of the most unique air-to-air kills credited to the squadron took place Feb. 14, 1991 during Operation Desert Storm. Captains Richard Bennett, pilot, and Daniel Bakke, weapon systems operator, scored the first air-to-air kill for an F-15E Strike Eagle.

A Special Forces team made an urgent call to an E-3 Sentry requesting assistance with three Iraqi Mi-24 Hind helicopter gunships in the area. The Airborne Warning and Control System contacted Captains Bennett and Bakke who were already airborne leading a flight of F-15Es during a Scud combat air patrol mission.

Captain Bennett brought "487" up to full military power—top speed without the use of afterburners. After breaking through the weather, the crew had to deal with Iraqi anti-aircraft artillery batteries. The crew picked up the three Mi-24 Hind helicopters on their target pod and observed that the Hinds were offloading troops at different points in an attempt to surround the Special Forces team.

The Strike Eagle crew decided to take out the lead helicopter with a GBU-10 while the helicopter was on the ground. If the Hind should take off again, the bomb would at least affect the troops in the immediate area. The crew dropped off the GBU-10 just as the helicopter picked up into a hover. The weapon systems officer kept lasing the target even though their radar showed the helicopter at 100 knots and gaining altitude.

Captain Bennett felt they had missed the target and began to ready an AIM-9 Sidewinder for a second shot. The crew then observed a flash of light; the explosion nearly vaporized the Iraqi helicopter gunship.

The Special Forces team estimated that the helicopter was at least 245 meters off the ground when it disintegrated in mid air. The other Mi-24 gunships bugged out, giving the Special Forces team a chance to move back to a secure location to be extracted.

Today, "487" is still assigned to the same squadron it made history with in 1991. It's the Chiefs' flagship and has a small green star adorned on the aircraft's port side representing that moment in the squadron's history. Alongside the prominent green star are current mission markings symbolizing strafing and air strikes flown against Anti-Afghanistan Forces.

Pilots and weapon system officers from the Chiefs are continuing to make history with the squadron's F-15E Strike Eagles, to include "487," fighting terror and building peace throughout Afghanistan."
(First published by *Air Force e-Publishing*, April 29, 2008.)

---

was in possession of WMD led to the order that the 4th Tactical Fighter Wing was to have at least one squadron ready to be deployed to the Persian Gulf. In late 2002, the 336th TFS was chosen to be the first unit deployed to Al Udeid Air Base in Qatar. In mid-January, 2003, a total of twenty-four F-15Es relocated to Qatar where they began combat preparations working with the Combined Air Operations Center at Prince Sultan Air Base in Saudi Arabia. Unfortunately, diplomatic issues between Qatar and the United States first had to be worked out before flying could finally resume on January 27.

The 336th flew numerous missions in support of OSW performing various reconnaissance and surveillance duties along with strike familiarization flights in which aircrews simulated attacks on potential targets located throughout Iraq. This enabled the aircrews to familiarize themselves with the local area and the applicable rules of engagement as well as proficiency in dealing with AWACS communications and flying over hostile territory.

Within a month, additional aircrews were sent in support of OSW and numbered four crew per plane. Most of the fresh pilots and WSOs were from the two non-deployable 333rd and 334th Tactical Fighter Squadrons at Seymour Johnson Air Force Base along with the 391st Tactical Fighter Squadron at Mountain

Although no F-15E has yet to achieve an air-to-air kill, technicalities may be put aside when it comes to the 335th Fighter Squadron's 89-0487. *USAF*

Home Air Force Base. Joining the 336th at Al Udeid in early March was the 335th Tactical Fighter Squadron. Toward the conclusion of OSW, the units were tasked with eliminating Iraqi air defenses near the Jordanian border along with the early warning radar network. This was necessary to allow U.S. Special Operations Forces' helicopters and equipment, along with F-16s, to operate out of Jordan.

The 335th and 336th were finally redeployed back to Seymour Johnson Air Force Base in mid-2003. They were replaced by the combat veteran 494th.

An F-15E Strike Eagle from the 335th Fighter Squadron, 4th Fighter Wing, based at Seymour Johnson Air Force Base displays the raw power of a multi-purpose air superiority aircraft. Despite the impressive display, the aircraft is far from fully loaded as it prepares to receive fuel from a KC-10A Extender cargo/tanker from the 763rd Expeditionary Air Refueling Squadron. The F-15E carries an AIM-120A AMRAAM on the outer pylons, a pair of AIM-9M Sidewinder missiles on the inside, four GBU-12 500-pound bombs, an AN/AAQ-28 (V) LITENING AT targeting pod on the right, and a LANTIRN on the left. *USAF*

CHAPTER FIVE

WEAPONS LOAD

TO BE AN EFFECTIVE FIGHTER, A SELECT type of ordnance must accompany the aircraft. As the AIM-7 Sparrow and AIM-9 Sidewinder matured, they found their way from the F-4 Phantom II of Vietnam to the pylons of the F-15. Radar systems aboard the Eagle also matured, enabling incredible accuracy for the air-to-air weapons load.

Once the F-15E Strike Eagle had taken to the skies, the arsenal of weapons utilized by the fighter increased four-fold, making it one of the most versatile fighters ever created. Capable of carrying bunker busters, guided and unguided conventional bombs, and cluster bombs, the F-15E can carry a larger payload than that of a World War II B-17 bomber.

WEAPONS LOAD F-15A-D

M61A1 20MM VULCAN CANNON

Loaded with a maximum of 940 rounds (or 600 on the F-15E) of 20mm munitions, the pneumatically or hydraulically driven, six-barrel, air-cooled, electronically activated Gatling gun allows the F-15 to engage adversaries in close quarter combat. One of the core justifications for the introduction of the F-15 Eagle was that the internal gun fires plutonium tipped rounds that can blast through some of the toughest armor found on any adversary aircraft.

The Vulcan gun is, by no means, a new weapon. Toward the end of World War II, the U.S. Army Air Force was looking to improve current gun technology. Scouring captured German weapons, such as the Mauser MG213C design, revealed the limitations of

The Gatling gun is capable of dispensing up to 940 rounds on the F-15C or 600 rounds on the Strike Eagle. It was thought there would no longer be a need for close-in weapons as dogfighting would become a thing of the past with beyond visual range (BVR) technology. Following the Korean and Vietnam Wars, every fighter aircraft produced has been equipped with a close-in weapons system. *USAF*

single barrel guns. In particular, the rate of fire and munitions feed were less than desirable.

As aircraft became faster, the rate of fire and potency of weaponry needed to advance as well. The Browning M2 heavy-barrel 50-caliber machine guns commonly used in World War II had a maximum firing rate of 1,200 rounds per minute and were becoming obsolete. The Army handed the challenge over to the General Electric Armament Division. The answer was to increase the number of barrels by reintroducing the Gatling gun, first invented in 1862

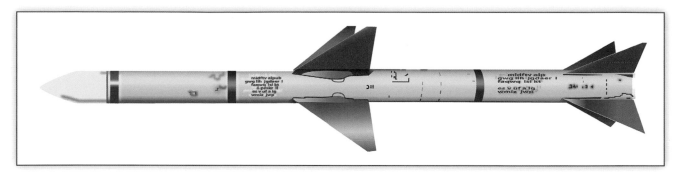

AIM-7 *Courtesy Raytheon*

by physician Richard Gatling. The rotating barrel concept proved impractical on older aircraft due to the additional power source needed for the barrel to revolve. With the advent of newer turbojet aircraft, the necessary power was no longer a concern.

In 1946, General Electric (GE) was given the contract for Project Vulcan. The concept was to lower the number of rounds per barrel, per minute, but multiply it over six barrels. Not only would this increase the total rounds per minute fired but reduce

The F-15's design provided for an assortment of weaponry. This Eagle shows off its four square-finned AIM-9 Sidewinders along with the four additional triangle-finned AIM-7 Sparrows. *USAF*

A pilot's point of view onboard an F-15C Eagle from the 123rd Fighter Squadron, Oregon Air National Guard , shows an AIM-7 Sparrow missile being launched. The missile's firing took place during exercise Combat Archer, a weapons system evaluation program hosted by the 83rd Fighter Weapons Squadron located at Tyndall Air Force Base, Florida. *USAF*

the heat generation and wear on each barrel. General Electric first fired the prototype designated T-171 in 1949 at a rate of 6,000 rounds per minute.

The gun was eventually named the Vulcan M61 and after a few modifications to solve misfeeding problems, changed to M61A1. Eventually, the design was sold to General Dynamics and was fitted to most U.S. fighters. It is currently manufactured by the Lockheed Martin Company.

Until recently, the Vulcan used the M50 rounds that came in a variety of applications including armor-piercing incendiary, high-explosive incendiary, and standard training rounds. Typical muzzle velocity of the M50 was approximately 3,380 feet per second.

The M61A1 was constructed with either an electric or a gas-driven barrel system. The GAU-4 is a self-powered system that extracts gas from four of the six barrels to maintain operation. Although the gas variant weighs an additional ten pounds, it requires no external power.

The latest version of the Vulcan, the M61A2, was modified to remove any non-essential components, reducing barrel thickness and replacing certain components with lighter weight materials in order to reduce the weight to a total of 202 pounds. The newest version can be found on the USN Boeing F/A-18E/F Super Hornet and the latest frontline fighter, the Lockheed Martin F-22 Raptor. The lighter-weight barrels allow for up to 6,600 rounds per minute and increased muzzle velocity to 3,450 feet per second firing PGU-28 rounds. The PGU-28 semi armor-piercing high-explosive incendiary round was introduced in 1988 and is now standard in the USN and USAF.

Despite the gun's service longevity, it is not without its shortcomings. European and Russian air forces chose the 30mm round due to its greater destructive impact while the United States selected the 20mm for increased overall firepower. With the production of the F-15, the use of 20mm rounds was not the USAF's first choice. Due to the relatively poor ballistic characteristics of the 20mm, the USAF spent an incredible amount of money to develop a gun capable of firing 25–30mm rounds—with little success.

AIM-7 SPARROW

One of the most successful and diverse air intercept missiles (AIM) created for air-to-air combat, the AIM-7 Sparrow, has found its way into three of

Two of the three F-15C Eagles from the 390th Fighter Squadron from Mountain Home Air Force Base, Idaho, fire AIM-7 Sparrowsat, a subscale aerial-target-drone MQM-107E Streaker, over the Gulf of Mexico during Combat Archer. The USAF air-to-air weapons system evaluation program was hosted by the 83rd Fighter Weapons Squadron. *USAF*

the five U.S. armed forces as well as North Atlantic Treaty Organization (NATO) forces. With platforms such as the Marine Corps F/A-18 Hornet, Navy F-14 Tomcat, and the Air Force F-15 and F-16 aircraft, the radar-guided air-to-air missile is all-weather and all-altitude capable. It has the ability to strike aircraft coming from any direction as well as missiles by using the four delta-shaped fins in the front for steering and the fixed rear fins for stability. The Sparrow's supersonic speed is provided by a dual-propulsion solid propellant rocket motor.

Target accuracy is obtained through the guidance and control section (GCS). This portion of the missile tracks a target using energy reflected from the subject in combination with data being received from the missile's fire control system. Calculating the difference

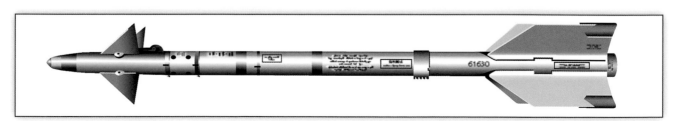

AIM-9M *Courtesy Raytheon*

between these two sources of information allows the Sparrow to determine position. Once the missile is within lethal range of the target it uses an active radar proximity fuze or a backup contact fuze to begin warhead detonation.

Despite the USAF's desire to rely heavily on the AIM-7 and AIM-9 during the Vietnam War, early models were far from dependable. Originally named project Hotshot, the Sparrow program began in 1946 and became operational in 1953. Initial use in Vietnam showed it to be practically useless toward the more agile communist aircraft. An attempt to improve the success rate led to the AIM-7E-2 dogfight variant.

Over the years, various improvements were made to keep up with the advancements of adversarial aircraft. The AIM/RIM-7E provided improved maneuverability for better dogfight interception as well as a reduction in minimum range restrictions. The AIM-7F utilized solid state circuitry, an improved warhead, and more powerful propulsion system along with a convenient modular design. The AIM/RIM-7R is the most current design and adds radio frequency and infrared seeker capability.

The primary medium-range missile for the newly introduced F-15 was the AIM-7F. Added to the USAF inventory in 1976, the F model was a complete rebuild over the previous E variant. To insure the missile was able to complement the new fighter, improved avionics were incorporated that allowed the warhead to be placed in the front of the missile, allowing for a larger motor, thus improving the long-range capability.

Additional modifications were made to the Sparrow missile in 1982, such as overall reliability and performance at low altitudes while encountering various ECM threats. In addition, the AIM-7M was outfitted with a much more lethal warhead. Since its operational status began in 1987, the M model has been the primary variant carried by the F-15 and F-16. With the development of the AIM-7F, the Sparrow took on a modular design consisting of six elements, the guidance and control section (GCS), rocket motor assembly, fuze booster, warhead assembly, rear waveguide assembly, and the wing and fin assembly.

The GCS enables the Sparrow to track a target by directing and stabilizing the missile as it constantly

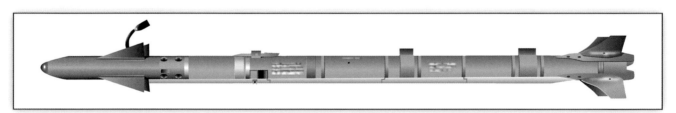

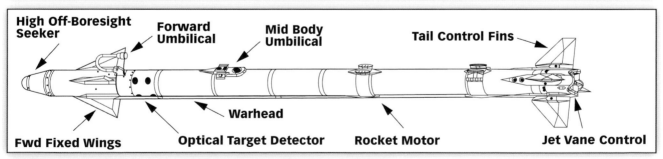

High Off-Boresight Seeker **Forward Umbilical** **Mid Body Umbilical** **Tail Control Fins**

Fwd Fixed Wings **Optical Target Detector** **Warhead** **Rocket Motor** **Jet Vane Control**

Courtesy Raytheon

AIM-9X Sidewinder Specifictaions		
Weight:	118 lb	85 kg
Length	119 in	3 m
Diameter:	5 in	12.7 cm
Fin Span:	17.5 in	44.45 cm
Wing Span:	13.9 in	35.31 cm

An F-15C Eagle assigned to Detachment 1, 28th Test Squadron, located at Nellis Air Force Base, maneuvers into a vertical climb. Its mission was to evaluate the short-range, heat-seeking, air-intercept AIM-9X Sidewinder missile. The Air Force Operational Test and Evaluation Center, Detachment 2, at Eglin Air Force Base, Florida, conducted the evaluation. *USAF*

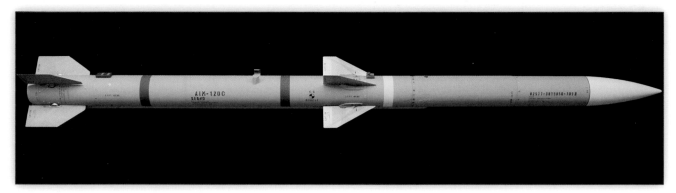

AIM-120 *Courtesy Raytheon*

reconfigures its course to target. Additionally, the GCS module is responsible for detonating the warhead by activating a radar proximity fuze or a backup contact fuze.

Designated MK-58, the rocket motors are dual-thrust, solid propellant units with two assemblies consisting of separate boost and sustain propellants in a side-by-side configuration. The combination of these case-bonded grain propellants enables the Sparrow increased range and supersonic speeds. The 2-, 3-, and 5-series AIM-7M/P modifications are specifically used for air-to-air combat with modified safety releases.

While technically part of the warhead assembly, the fuze booster module is responsible for igniting the main warhead charge. In order to provide an additional amount of safety to ordnance personnel, the second generation MK-38 fuze booster was designed to melt instead of detonate when exposed to high heat.

Located between the GCS components, the warhead contains the fuze assembly that is connected electrically to the GCS section by a safe-arm device. As the pilot signals the missile for launch, an electrical charge activates the arming mechanism. Once fired, the arming cycle is begun by a thrust-activated mechanism in the safe-arm device unit. Acceleration of the missile enables the arming rotor to turn, thus aligning the explosive components and disabling the shorting circuit completing the arming process. An impact switch located in the GCS, or the active radio frequency fuze circuit in the GCS, sends a pulse enabling detonation.

The two-part rear waveguide assembly connects the radio frequency circuitry to the GCS via an external antenna in the front of the missile. Utilizing a tunnel cable running the length of the missile, the rear portion of the assembly contains the main antenna.

Critical to the flight performance of the AIM-7, the wing and fin assembly consists of four wings and four fins. Toward the front of the missile, the wings attach near the GCS assembly. Used for stability purposes, the fins at the back of the missile are mounted on quick-attach fittings in a dovetail configuration inline with the delta-shaped wings in the front.

AIM-9 SIDEWINDER

With an almost identical history to that of the AIM-7 Sparrow, the Raytheon AIM-9 Sidewinder was developed as a highly maneuverable, supersonic, heat-seeking, air-to-air missile. Designated the AIM-9B, official production of the Sidewinder began in 1956 with the prototype AIM-9A having successfully shot down an aerial drone three years prior. Initially developed for the USN for fleet air defense, the USAF eventually adopted the design for use by fighter aircraft. The decision was not without concern as the USAF insisted on challenging the capabilities of the AIM-9 against the AIM-4 Falcon already in use. After a fly-off in June 1955, the USAF was convinced of the Sidewinder's capabilities.

Potential of an air-to-air missile was realized on September 24, 1958, when Taiwanese F-86F Sabres downed eleven Chinese MiG-15s using Sidewinders supplied by the USN. Despite the Chinese Nationalist's aerial victories, the AIM-9 wasn't without its shortcomings. The initial production model lacked nighttime or head-on attack capabilities. Furthermore, it could not engage targets close to the ground.

The AIM-9E, a modified B, was the first official USAF model incorporating a slightly longer nose cone and improved seeker with thermoelectric cooling. Maneuverability was increased with a new, larger strake design allowing the missile to turn at a rate of sixteen degrees per second. Use of the AIM-9B/E Sparrows in Vietnam led to twenty-three air-to-air kills by USAF aircraft. The USN added to the kill rate with their variant, the AIM-9D/G. The total combined air-to-air kills during the war totaled eighty-two.

The USN AIM-9H variant eliminated the use of vacuum tubes in exchange for solid-state circuitry and demonstrated even greater maneuverability increasing the turn rate to twenty degrees per second. The USAF

adopted the AIM-9J as a replacement for the E model. Unlike the Navy's H model, the J still favored some use of the vacuum tube circuitry, but did replace a few components with solid state technology. Unique to the AIM-9J were the double-canard, square-tipped control surfaces. As deliveries of the AIM-9J began in 1977, the introduction of the F-15 placed the J model specifically for the Eagle and later rotated into service with other Sidewinder-compatible aircraft.

The USN and USAF finally began to work together on the design of the AIM-9L, improving tracking ability and adding a more powerful MK-38 solid-propellant motor. The most notable advancement was the implementation of the all-aspect capability that

This is an artist's concept of an F-15 Eagle launching a Raytheon version of the AMRAAM. Hughes was eventually awarded the contract; however, Raytheon became the follow-on producer of the missile. Raytheon ultimately bought out Hughes and is now the sole supplier of the AMRAAM. *USAF*

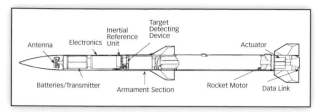

AMRAAM AIM-120C-7 Specifications		
Length:	12 ft.	3.65 cm
Diameter:	7 in	17.8 cm
Wing Span:	17.5 in	44.5 cm
Fin Span:	17.6 in	44.7 cm
Weight:	356 lb	161.5 kg
Warhead:	45 lb	20.5 kg
Guidance:	Active radar	
Fuzing:	Proximity and contact	
Launcher:	Rail and eject	

Courtesy Raytheon

allowed for improved maneuverability and guidance control. Beginning production in 1976, the AIM-9L with all-aspect capability was the first generation Sidewinder capable of engaging a target head-on as well as from any other angle. Other improvements included increased lethality and resistance to ECM. The AIM-9L managed to change combat tactics as the need to dogfight and maneuver to opponent's six o'clock position was no longer necessary.

Further advancements to the Sidewinder soon followed. The AIM-9M incorporated an improved guidance system, reduced smoke motor, better countermeasures resistance (infrared counter-countermeasures), and improved maintainability. A USAF sponsored project, the AIM-9P was a

modification of the AIM-9J/N that enabled allied countries unable to afford or not allowed access to the AIM-9L/M. Similarly, the AIM-9S is a stripped down variant of the AIM-9M without the infrared counter-countermeasures.

The short-lived AIM-9R featured improved infrared technology allowing for better midday success rates. After only two years, funding was cancelled for the Romeo variant and a replacement for the AIM-9M became priority. In 1991, efforts to develop a replacement became known as the AIM-9X program with both Raytheon and Hughes as contenders. Upon completing the demonstration-validation competition, Hughes was offered the contract in December 1996. Eventually, Hughes was bought out by Raytheon, and the AIM-9X was manufactured under the Raytheon name. Firing trials began in 1998 with a successful downing of a QF-4 drone in 1999. Evaluation units from the USN and USAF began receiving the AIM-9X in 2002, with acceptance and full production beginning in May 2004.

The AIM-9X features a new smaller design enabling it to be contained within the weapons bays of the F-22 Raptor and Lockheed Martin F-35 Joint Strike Fighter. Using the same MK-36 propulsion system along with the WDU-17/B warhead of the AIM-9M, the AIM-9X utilizes a completely new guidance system incorporating an imaging infrared seeker. Of great importance were compatibility issues with other emerging technologies such as the joint helmet-mounted cueing system used for advanced targeting acquisition, as well as the existing launch rails (LAU-7/A, LAU-127/A, 128/A, and 129/A series).

AGM-65 *Courtesy Raytheon*

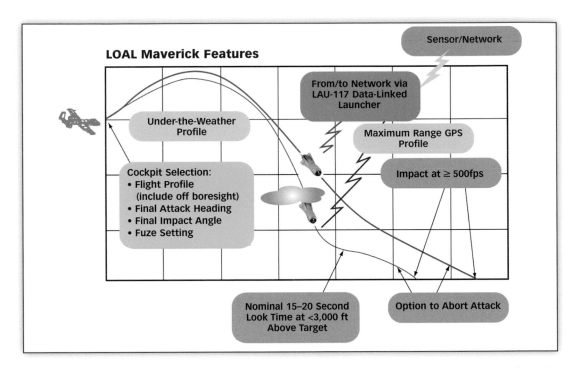

AIM-120 AMRAAM SLAMMER

The AIM-120 Slammer is an advanced medium-range air-to-air missile (AMRAAM) with all-weather, beyond-visual-range capability. Able to reach Mach 4 and strike targets at a distance of forty miles, the AIM-120 utilizes active radar tracking, proportional navigation guidance, and active radio frequency target detection.

A study conducted in 1975, suggested aerial threats should be engaged at distances further than what the AIM-7 Sparrow and AIM-9 Sidewinder were capable of, preferably up to the forty-mile range. As a result, the AMRAAM program was developed due to a joint service operational requirement for a missile that could be used as a follow on to the AIM-7 and AIM-9. Development of the AIM-120 was the result of a joint agreement between the United States and other NATO nations, similar to the General Dynamics F-16 Falcon program of the same time period.

By February 1979, the AMRAAM program completed its conceptual phase. Two contractors were selected to further develop the weapon, Hughes Aircraft Company and Raytheon. During the validation phase, both companies produced hardware capable of meeting the USAF and USN recommendations. In December 1981, Hughes Aircraft Company was awarded the contract.

By 1987, both companies were able to produce the AIM-120 with Raytheon being the follower producer. The USN and USAF fired approximately two hundred missiles at various locations such as Eglin Air Force Base, NAS Point Mugu, and White Sands Missile Range. The USAF declared the missile's operational capability in September 1991, while the USN waited until F/A-18C/D integration in 1993.

With the merging of Hughes Aircraft Company and Raytheon Systems, the military took on a new approach to acquiring AIM-120 units. Typically, a dual-source competitive contract is initiated, as had been the case with prior orders. Recognizing potential monetary savings, the government moved toward a more commercial business strategy called AMRAAM Vision 2000. The government's Lot 12 purchase was for a total of 813 units with 173 going to the USAF and 120 to the USN. An additional 520 AIM-120s were sent to foreign customers. In all, the AMRAAM Vision 2000 arrangement saved the USAF and USN more than $150 million dropping the price from $340,000 per unit to $299,000.

Currently in production are the AIM-120B and C models. Both models have the ability to be reprogrammed using common field-level memory reprogramming equipment while the A model required a hardware change for each reprogramming. All models, including the A variant, are capable of

The AGM-65 Maverick can target almost any surface threat such as SAM sites, ships, and armored vehicles. Utilizing an infrared image guidance system or an interchangeable laser seeker, the weapon can be either self or manually guided. Even in adverse weather or nighttime conditions, the Maverick finds its way to the target. If misdirected, it automatically disengages the warhead, flies above the target, and becomes a dud. *Courtesy Raytheon*

being carried by F-15, F-16, and F/A-18 aircraft. Modifications to the fin design making the control surfaces smaller enable the C model to be carried internally on the F-22 Raptor.

Similar to the smaller AIM-7 and AIM-9 series are the modules incorporated into the AIM-120's design such as the weapons guidance unit (WGU), weapons detonation unit (WDU), weapons propulsion unit, weapons control unit (WCU), and the wing and fin assembly.

Contained within the front portion of the AIM-120 is the WGU consisting of a servo, seeker, transmitter-receiver, electronics unit, target detection device, inertial reference unit, harness, and frame structure. The AIM-120B uses the WGU-41/B guidance unit while the AIM-120C is equipped with the WGU-44/B unit. Just behind the WGU section is the warhead (WDU-33/B). The WDU includes the safe-arm fuze device (MK-3 Mod 5) and the MK 44 booster. Included in the external portion of the warhead section is the forward hook and hangar.

The propulsion unit is where the integral rocket motor, blast tube and exit cone are all located. Using a reduced smoke propellant, the solid-fuel rocket motor is made up of a hydroxyl-terminated, polybutadiene propellant in a boost sustain configuration. Wings are attached to the external portion of the WDU module. The WCU is located toward the rear. Much of what

makes the weapon safe is located in the WCU, such as the thermally initiated venting system containing an out-of-line device that allows the rocket motor to vent without exploding. Another safety feature found in the WCU is the ability to reset after missile launch. Set to activate following nine to thirteen G-tolerance of inertia, the reset feature prevents the missile from detonating during the course of target tracking. This may be experienced due to aerodynamic pressure possibly enabling the thermally initiated venting system.

Providing for flight control, the wing and fin assemblies remained the same for the AIM-120A and B models and are completely interchangeable should they need replacing. The AIM-120C incorporates a clipped wing design to facilitate the internal storage of the Slammer on the F-22 Raptor. The stationary flight surfaces in the rear of the missile are attached with ball fasteners for quick removal while the wings in the front are the only movable control surfaces.

Although the F-15A-D and E models are capable of carrying the Slammer, it is not a commonly employed part of the Eagle's weapons package. The first time the missile was slung beneath the wings of an F-15 was during Operation Desert Storm. It was later returned to combat with the F-15 for Operation Enduring Freedom. To date, the AIM-120 has never been fired during combat from an Eagle.

F-15E "STRIKE EAGLE" SPECIFIC WEAPONS PACKAGE

AGM-65 MAVERICK

A self-guided, air-to-ground missile, the AGM-65 is used primarily to attack high-value targets such as armored vehicles, ships, SAM sites and communications facilities. Being a self-guided weapon, or launch and leave, once fired the pilot can immediately track another target, take evasive action, or fire another weapon as the AGM-65 continues to guide itself through impact.

Introduced to the USAF in August 1972, the Maverick was originally destined for the Fairchild-Republic A-10 Thunderbolt II and later configured for use on the F-16 and F-15E.

The AGM-65A consisted of an electro-optical television guidance system. Using a cockpit television screen, the pilot can see what the missile sees. Once the target was positioned in the crosshairs, the pilot then "fired-and–forgot," leaving the missile's artificial intelligence to seek the target. The Bravo model allowed the pilot to magnify the target on-screen, enabling the missile to track smaller targets more accurately

Adding an imaging infrared guidance system, the AGM-65D, enabled the missile to lock on to targets despite adverse weather conditions during day or night. When older A-10s did not receive navigable infrared imaging systems, pilots used the visual systems of the AGM-65D for poor weather guidance and improved nighttime flying abilities.

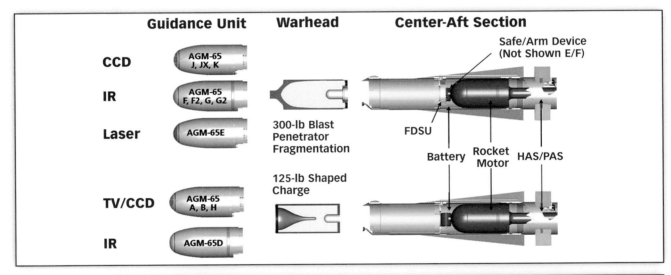

AGM-65 Maverick Specifications

Length:	98.0 in		249 cm	
Wing Span:	28.5 in		72 cm	
Diameter:	12.0 in		30.5 cm	
Fuze:	Contact, Selectable Delays			
Weight:	125-lb Shaped Charge Warhead			
	D (IR)		485 lb	220 kg
	H (TV)		466 lb	211 kg
	300-lb Blast Fragmentation Penetrator Warhead			
	E (Laser)		645 lb	293 kg
	F, F2, G, G2, (IR)		670 lb	304 kg
	J, JX, K (TV)		654 lb	297 kg
	Single-Rail Launcher			
	LAU-117		135 lb	61 kg

Courtesy Raytheon

116

AGM-130 *Courtesy Raytheon*

Unlike the laser-guided C variant that never made it into production, the AGM-65E successfully incorporated a laser guidance system for use with the U.S. Marine Corps. The USN AGM-65E/F utilized an interchangeable infrared or laser seeker with a larger warhead for use against high-value targets. The F model uses a 300-pound warhead while the USMC variant utilizes a smaller, but more concentrated 125-pound shaped charged unit.

The laser variant requires a laser designator that can either be airborne or ground based. The laser designator paints the target for the duration of the missile's flight. Should the missile lose acquisition of the laser, a safety feature enables the AGM-65E to fly above the target, deactivate the warhead and become a dud.

In an attempt to upgrade AGM-65s that had been placed in cold storage, the USAF installed improved charge couple device imaging chips on B models but found that modifying the G model with its larger 300-pound warhead was more practical. The AGM-65G differed from the D model by simply upgrading the guidance system to track larger targets and employing the larger warhead. The program upgrade resulted in the AGM-65K.

AGM-130

Lacking a NATO slang name, the AGM-130 was originally designed for use on the F-15E as an air-to-surface missile capable of striking targets from either a low or high-altitude position. The missile is capable of destroying moving targets from a 15–40 NM range and can be retargeted if necessary by using an inertial navigation guidance system aided by the use of global positioning system (GPS) satellites. In addition to GPS, the missile also uses a television or infrared seeker with man-in-the-loop guidance. A relatively large weapon, the AGM-130A makes use of a 2,000-pound general-purpose warhead and is essentially a powered version of the guided bomb unit-15 (GBU-15).

Equipped with an advanced charged couple device or infrared seeker, a visual representation of the target can be viewed by the launch aircraft as seen by the weapon via the AXQ-14 data-link system. With a clear view of the target by the rear seat WSO, the target can be locked on prior to or after launch as well as manually steered through use of the data link.

Due to the relatively long range of the AGM-130, low-altitude, long-range firing tactics have proven most successful. Able to fly using glide-powered glide phases, the missile receives constant navigational updates through its GPS system. Once the powered flight phase of the rocket is no longer needed and retargeting is unnecessary, the solid fuel motor can be discarded and the missile guided to its target.

The AGM-130 development program began in 1984 as an attempt to improve the capabilities of the GBU-15. Ten years later, the AGM-130A came to be, shortly followed by yet another advancement, the AGM-130 midcourse guidance missile. The midcourse guidance variant allows for less human input, enabling

This F-15E Strike Eagle, assigned to the 494th Fighter Squadron, Royal Air Force, Lakenheath, releases a custom-painted AGM-130 missile over the Utah Test and Training Range. The action was part of exercise Combat Hammer, a weapon system evaluation program conducted at Hill Air Force Base, Utah. *USAF*

the WSO to concentrate on other threats in an otherwise intense environment. Taking that logic to the next step is the job of the slightly smaller AGM-130LW (lightweight) able to be launched from a single-seat aircraft such as the F-16 as an all-weather, long-range weapon.

AGM-154 JSOW

Developed as an air-to-ground joint standoff weapon (JSOW), the AGM-154 can be fired from outside the range of enemy defenses. The JSOW falls within the 1,000-pound class of munitions weighing between 1,000 and 1,500 pounds depending on the mission and has a length of just over thirteen feet. Typical load for the AGM-154A consists of 145 BLU-97 bomblets designed to disperse over a 30,000-square-foot area.

Belonging to the family of kinetically efficient weaponry, the munition is designed to glide to its target. Depending on altitude, the AIM-154 has a range of fifteen nautical miles if fired from its minimum altitude and up to forty miles if launched from a higher cruising altitude.

Once fired, the JSOW is known as a launch-and-leave weapon, incorporating a GPS system that will guide it to the target regardless of adverse weather or nighttime conditions. Following initial launch, GPS is used and within ten seconds of reaching the target, an infrared imaging and communications data-link takes over for terminal homing.

Testing of the weapon by the USAF began in March 1996 at Eglin Air Force Base, Florida, utilizing an F-16. Although results by the Development Test & Evaluation (DT&E) proved less than desirable, it had

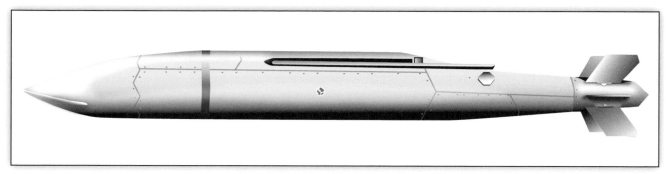

AGM-154 *Courtesy Raytheon*

nothing to do with the interface between the aircraft and weapon but rather a component within the JSOW manufactured by a contractor other than the Texas Instruments Defense Systems and Electronics team. When the USN began testing under the Operational Evaluation (OPEVAL) program in February 1997, results showed a 96 percent success rate.

The AGM-154A began production under a $65.9 million contract for the USN under the low rate initial production program with a B model variant entering production in fiscal year 2000. Early units were provided to the Navy for use aboard the USS *Nimitz* and USS *Eisenhower*, however it was the USS *Carl Vinson*'s air wing that enabled the weapon to first

A remotely captured image shows bomblets released from an AGM-130. Bomblet dispersion enables the weapon to inflict maximum damage upon the target. Equipping the weapon with many types of bomblets allows use on a variety of targets. *Courtesy Raytheon*

see combat while patroling the skies of Southern Iraq on January 25, 1999.

The combat readiness of the JSOW was attributed to a massive effort by members of Raytheon, having taken over Texas Instruments in January 1997. Working with the China Lake Naval Air Weapons Center, Weapons Division, personnel were sent to the USS *Carl Vinson* in the Persian Gulf to reprogram initial production JSOWs for applicable missions. In less than ten days from the initial programming request, the weapon was used in combat and its lethality was confirmed only days after the USN announced the JSOW as being operational.

While the JSOW has remained primarily a USN weapon, the effectiveness didn't go unnoticed by the USAF. Modifications to the AGM-154B and the USN proprietary AGM-154C include improved aircraft-to-weapon communication using the MIL-STD-1760 interface. An anti-spoofing module was also integrated along with an improved GPS unit under a June 2000 contract through Raytheon.

The latest model to be developed is the JSOW Unitary (JSOW-C) variant that went into full production in December 2004. The JSOW-C was used against installations such as hardened bunkers and radar sites making it the first U.S. weapon to use BAE's two-stage Broach package enabling fragmentation, blast, and penetration capability.

AGM-158 JOINT AIR TO SURFACE STANDOFF MISSILE (JASSM)

Also in the 1,000-pound class is the low observable, conventionally armed, joint air to surface standoff missile (JASSM) designed to destroy high-value targets inclusive of aircraft shelters, bunkers, and underground command posts while remaining outside enemy defenses. Armed with a WDU-42/B penetrating warhead containing 240 pounds of insensitive explosive dubbed AFX-757, the JASSM uses autonomous guidance and automatic target recognition for improved accuracy and potent penetration.

Initially, the DoD was calling for a tri-service standoff attack missile, but due to escalating costs and eventual cancellation of the program, a substitute was urgently needed. The result was a joint effort between the USN and USAF to create the JASSM, a survivability standoff weapon capable of destroying a variety of deep interdiction targets.

Classified as a precision cruise missile, the AGM-158 is capable of targeting both fixed and relocatable targets by flying autonomously over a circuitous route at low-level. A midcourse anti-jam GPS and inertial navigation system will guide the missile toward the target. Once the missile is within critical range, approximately eight seconds, an imaging infrared seeker and a target recognition system will provide final aim point detection and strike tracking.

The JASSM program was approached by seven different contractors as a result of an RFP. One of them, McDonnell Douglas, was awarded a two-year, program definition and risk reduction contract on June 17, 1996. Eventually the development contract was awarded to Lockheed Martin in April 1998. By February 1999, testing of the $300,000 weapon began at Eglin Air Force Base as well as the White Sands Missile Range in New Mexico. Despite a three-month program test suspension due to target acquisition failure in October 2002, and increasing production costs, the program eventually continued. In 2002, the JASSM began a low rate initial production program with a total of seventy-six missiles being built for the USAF with deliveries beginning in April 2003.

Beginning production in 2003, the JASSM-ER (extended-range) variant enabled the weapon to cruise for over five hundred nautical miles. Incorporating a more efficient engine and greater internal fuel capacity, engineers at Lockheed Martin managed to include the improvements without modifying the external dimensions, greatly reducing potential increased development costs.

Other upgrades to the JASSM system include utilizing a multimode warhead and a modified maneuvering airframe capable of producing a high-performance submunition. The JASSM P-LOCAAS-DM P3I can also be modified depending on the rigidity of the target by incorporating an aerostable slug, long rod penetrator, or a fragment-based warhead. In place of the conventional motor, the LOCAAS will use a small turbojet engine capable of sustaining flight for up to thirty minutes, increasing the weapon's flexibility.

VARIANT	GUIDANCE	PAYLOAD	AFT
AGM-154A (BLU-97)	GUIDANCE COMPUTER	BLU-97 SUBMUNITIONS	FLIGHT CONTROL SYSTEM
AGM-154A-1 (BLU-111)	GUIDANCE COMPUTER	BLU-111 BLAST/FRAG	FLIGHT CONTROL SYSTEM
AGM-154B	GUIDANCE COMPUTER	BLU-108 SUBMUNITIONS	FLIGHT CONTROL SYSTEM
AGM-154C	GUIDANCE COMPUTER IIR SEEKER	BROACH BLAST/FRAG/ PENETRATING	FLIGHT CONTROL SYSTEM

JSOW Specifications

Length:	160 in	(4.1 m)
Weight:	1,050 lb	(475 kg) Depends on variant

Aircraft Compatibility:
- F-16, F-15E, F/A-18, B-2, B-52, P-3, F-35 (JSF), JAS 39 Gripen, Eurofighter 2000, Tornado
- Multiple carriage capable on BRU-55/BRU-57 twin launchers
- MIL-STD 1553/1760 and NATO STANAG 3837 AA interface for full capability

Range (unpowered):
- Low altitude 500-ft launch 12 nm (22km)
- High altitude 40,000-ft launch 70 nm maximum kinematic range (130 km)

Range (powered):
- ~155 nm (290 km)

Range (powered):
- BLU-97   Combined effects bomblets
- BLU-108   Sensor-fused submunitions
- 500-lb BROACH   Blast/fragmentation and/or penetrating warhead
                Demonstrated 5-ft (1.5-m) concrete penetration in testing
- 500-lb BLU-111 Unitary blast/fragmentaion warhead

Courtesy Raytheon

An F-15E from the 46th Test Wing, 40th Flight Test Squadron, based at Eglin Air Force Base, Florida, is armed with an AGM-154 JSOW. The USAF studies flight characteristics prior to weapons deployment to see if the aircraft is capable of safely dropping the weapon with no adverse effects. *USAF*

B61 THERMONUCLEAR BOMB

The most versatile and plentiful nuclear weapon ever built, the B61 was specifically designed to be delivered to the target via USAF, USN, and NATO aircraft at almost any operable altitude and above speeds of Mach 2. Developed by the Department of Energy's Los Alamos National Laboratory in New Mexico, the weapon was designed to be carried internally or externally and dropped from an altitude as low as fifty feet by nearly two dozen different aircraft types. Equipped with a twenty-four-foot, Kevlar ribbon-type parachute, the 700-pound weapon can either be deployed as a free-fall unit or parachute retarded. Upon deployment of the chute, the B61's forward momentum is slowed from over 1,000 miles per hour to just 65 miles per hour in less than three seconds followed by either an air burst or ground burst. Additionally, the weapon can be programmed to provide a laydown period, a pause before detonation that enables the delivery aircraft to safely vacate the area.

First produced in 1966 to replace the aging B28, B43, and B67 nuclear units, the B61 was designed to be a relatively lightweight and versatile thermonuclear weapon. Depending on the variation and warhead type, the twelve-foot-long unit weighs an average of approximately 750 pounds. Originally the nose mounted radar consisted of vacuum-tube electronics and by 2000, in cooperation with AlliedSignal, the Department of Energy began upgrading to the solid-state MC4033 radar.

Since 1966, the B61 has been in constant improvement with more than a half-dozen modifications being applied. In 2002, the B61 casing and aerodynamics were scrutinized and tested. Fin design was modified to not only reduce vortices but

Mk-82 *Courtesy Raytheon*

also predict what effects aerodynamics would have on the weapons trajectory and flight characteristics. That same year, enhancements were made to all B61 units in the 3, 4, and 10 models to insure the safety and reliability of the weapon.

MK-80 SERIES LOW DRAG GENERAL PURPOSE (LDGP) BOMB

The Snakeye is the primary weapon used in most bombing operations where the intent is simply to blow up the target. Originally used in 1964, the Snakeye was designed to be relatively aerodynamic, containing approximately forty-five percent of its total weight as explosive, utilizing both conical or retarded tail fins along with fuzes in both the nose and tail. This design enabled the weapon to be dropped from an aircraft at low altitude without the fear of it being hit by exploding bomb fragments. The Mk-80 series proved its worth during Operation Desert Storm when various designs were dropped from every type of fixed wing attack aircraft against targets such as SCUDs, SAM sites, AAA sites, bunkers, radar installations, armored vehicles, and much more.

The Mk-82 is a 500-pound general purpose bomb typically outfitted with an M904 mechanical fuze on the nose and either a mechanical M905 tail fuze or FMU-113 radar proximity air-burst fuze. The Mk-83 steps up to the 1,000-pound class and is equipped with the BSU-85/B high drag tail assembly or ballute. Resembling a balloon-parachute, the high-strength nylon fabric ballute fans out creating an enormous amount of drag enabling the bomb to slow down rapidly at low altitudes and allowing the aircraft to depart the fragmentation area.

The Mk-84 doubles the potency of the Mk-83 and was primarily dropped by F-15Es, F-16s, and F-111Fs during Operation Desert Storm. Of the 12,000 Mk-84s dropped, fewer than 1,000 were from other aircraft.

BOMB LIVE UNIT SERIES OF WEAPONS (BLU)

The F-15E can carry a number of bomb live units (BLU) designed to penetrate underground installations, hardened targets, weapons storage facilities, and more. The concept is for the bomb casing to remain intact until after penetration whereby exploding in closer proximity.

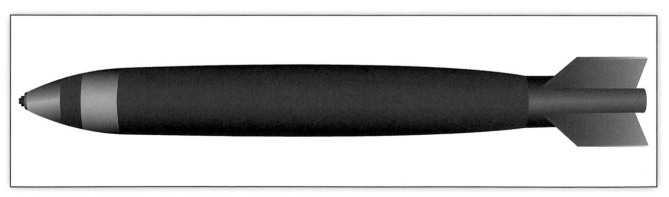

Mk-83 *Courtesy Raytheon*

The BLU-109 is a 2,000-pound bomb developed by Lockheed Martin in 1985, nicknamed "HAVE VOID." It has become the primary weapon for allied naval and air forces. United States Air Force specifications called for a weapon that could penetrate six feet of reinforced concrete and detonate via a delayed-action fuze. Containing 550 pounds of PBNX-109 explosive material, National Forge Company was awarded the contract by Lockheed Martin in 1986 to machine the hardened steel warhead. When combined with various GBU tail kits, the BLU-109 becomes a special purpose guided bomb unit (GBU).

Containing a smaller warhead than the BLU-109, the BLU-110 incorporates a 1,000-pound forged steel casing warhead and can be converted into a JDAM munition. Similar to GBUs, the JDAM tail kits enable dumb free-fall bombs to become accurately guided smart bombs. Both the BLU-110 and BLU-111 thermally protected bombs are identical to the MK82 and MK83 with the exception of having a more powerful explosive warhead. Should the MK82 and MK83 be filled with the potent PBNX-109 filler, they are renamed BLU-110 and BLU-111.

The BLU-111 is an even smaller weapon containing a 500-pound warhead most closely resembling the MK82 but with a more potent explosive compound. Like the BLU-110, the BLU-111 is a thermally protected bomb capable of carrier operations. The thermal technology comes into play by protecting the weapon from premature detonation should the unit become engulfed in a shipboard fuel fire.

The success of a bomb, either guided or free-fall, is based on various physical properties such as the center of gravity, overall weight, aerodynamic shape, and inertia. Prior to any weapon being carried on an aircraft, complex testing must be done with each applicable airframe. Due to escalating costs incurred in the development and certification process, the BLU-116 was designed to identically emulate the already certified BLU-109. Furthermore, guidance packages already in existence can easily be adapted with little or no additional modifications.

Having a warhead twice the size of the BLU-109, the 4,000-pound BLU-116 is the latest addition to the armed forces inventory of hard target penetrating bombs. Also designated as an advanced unitary penetrator, the BLU-116 was the product of an Air Force Research Laboratory Munitions Directorate. With a development cost of less than $8 million, Eglin Air Force Base's Precision Strike System Program Office approved the advanced unit penetrator in less than three years.

Success of the BLU-116 is due mainly to the 1,700-pound warhead encased in an aerodynamic shroud and activated via a hard target smart fuze. The larger warhead enables the weapon to penetrate extremely dense multilayer underground targets up to twice the density of the BLU-109. Penetration is accomplished by the shroud stripping away upon initial impact of the target and a smaller explosive charge reduces collateral damage. Proof of the weapon's precision was demonstrated during Operation Allied Force.

Like other BLU weapons, the BLU-116 can be modified by adding a multitude of guidance packages containing GPS units enabling it to become a precision target munition. Proven guidance packages include the GBU-10, GBU-15, GBU-24, GBU-27, JDAM, and AGM-130 kits.

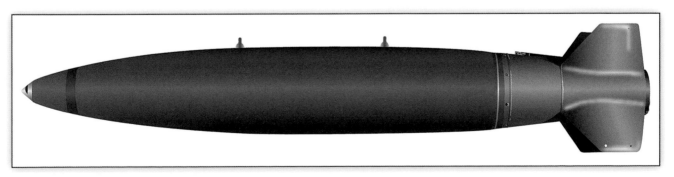

Mk-84 *Courtesy Raytheon*

Specifications		Aircraft Compatibility
GBU-10		
Warhead:	MK-84	A-6, A-7, F-4, F-5, F-14, F-15, F-16, F/A-18, F-111, F-117
Weight:	2081 lb	
Length:	170 in	
Guidance:	MAU-169	
Airfoil Group:	MXU-651/B	
GBU-16		
Warhead:	MK-83	A-4, A-6, A-7, F-4, F-5, F-14, F-15, F-16, F/A-18, F-111, Harrier, Jaguar, Mirage III, Mirage 2000, Super Etendard
Weight:	1092 lb	
Length:	145 in	
Guidance:	MAU-169	
Airfoil Group:	MXU-667/B	
GBU-12		
Warhead:	MK-82	A-4, A-6, A-7, F-4, F-5, F-14, F-15, F-16, F/A-18, AMX, Harrier, Jaguar, Mirage 2000, Mirage F-1, Tornado
Weight:	611 lb	
Length:	131 in	
Guidance:	MAU-169	
Airfoil Group:	MXU-650/B	

Courtesy Raytheon

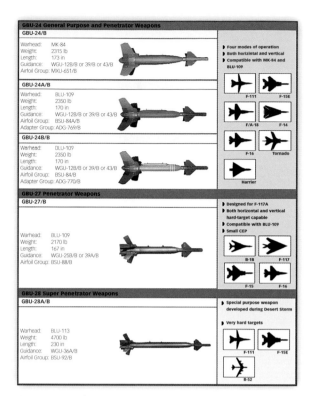

Courtesy Raytheon

GUIDED BOMB UNITS (GBU)

Mating with the BLU-109 is the GBU-10 laser guidance kit containing an MK-84 2,000-pound bomb. The GBU-10 Paveway II bomb relies on an operator-illuminated target using a laser designator to hone in on its mark. The original Paveway I series with fixed wings was retired in favor of the Paveway II's folding wings, improved detector optics with a greater field of view and sensitivity along with an injection-molded casing allowing for greater cost savings and overall weight reduction. The GBU-10 weighs almost 2,600 pounds with a length of just over fourteen feet and a cost (USAF) of $23,700 each.

Introduced in 1968 as a replacement to the electro-optical GBU-8, the GBU-10 first saw action in North Vietnam tasked with destroying the highly fortified Doumer Bridge in May 1972. With great success, the weapon took out the bridge utilizing sixteen F-4 Phantoms compared to the nine failed previous missions five years earlier, using the older bomb guidance technology. Nearly twenty years later, the GBU-10 was again used with great success during Operation Desert Storm recording a seventy-eight percent hit accuracy.

Also in the Paveway II class, the 800-pound, 11-foot-long GBU-12 contains a 500-pound Mk-82 warhead. During Operation Desert Storm, GBU-12s reached an eighty-eight percent success rate. A newer version of the weapon is the Enhanced-GBU-12, or EGBU-12, capable of operating in all-weather conditions as a dual-mode guided bomb. Taking advantage of GPS technology, the weapon can offer precision guidance to the target or can act upon a laser guidance system to hone in on mobile threats.

The GBU-15 was initially a step back to the electro-optical system enabling the WSO to guide the bomb via a real-time monitor located on the instrument panel. Like the GBU-10, the GBU-15 makes use of an Mk-84 or a BLU-109 dumb bomb yet adds a data-link controlled system allowing it cruise until guidance is taken over by either the WSO or central computer upon seeing the target. Imagery is provided through either a video system or infrared camera in the nose of the kit.

Currently, the only USAF aircraft able to carry the GBU-15 is the F-15E Strike Eagle, employing the weapon as either a direct or indirect attack weapon with standoff capability. The now-retired F-111F was, at one time, the only other USAF aircraft certified to launch the GBU-15. During Operation Desert Storm, seventy-one converted GBU-15s were used to prevent oil from spilling into the Persian Gulf by sealing oil pipeline manifolds sabotaged by Saddam Hussein. All bombs used to thwart Hussein's efforts were deployed by F-111F Aardvark aircraft.

Initially developed in 1974, the electro-optical design was approved and put into service by

Paveway™ Comparison				
	Paveway™ II LGB	**Paveway™ III LGB**	**Enhanced Paveway™ III DMLGB**	**Enhanced Paveway™ III DMLGB**
Weapons	GBU-10: MK-84, BLU-109 GBU-12: MK-82, BANG 250 GBU-16: MK-83 GBU MK-81, BANG 125 UK MK-13/18/20	GBU-22: MK-82 GBU-24: MK-84, BANG-109 BLU-116, CPE 800 GBU-28: BLU-113	EGBU-10: MK-84, BLU-109 EGBU-12: MK-82 EGBU-16: MK-83 Enhanced Paveway™ II DMLGB Lot 1: MK-13/20 Enhanced Paveway™ II DMLGB Lot 4 (Paveway™ IV)	GBU-24: MK-84, BLU-116, BLU-109 GBU-27: BLU-109 GBU-28: BLU-113, BLU-122 Enhanced Paveway™ II DMLGB (UK): BLU-109
Description	Combat-tested laser guidance features pinpoint accuracy and low cost	Combat-proven design for low-level, long-range delivery	Low cost combined with dual-mode laser/ GPS guidance greatly increases envelope of legacy Paveway™ II LGB. Combat proven	Adds GPS guidance to low-altitude/ long-range capability of Paveway™ III LGB. Flight path optimized for penetrator warhead. Combat proven
Method of Guidance	Laser	Laser	Independent dual-mode laser or GPS/INS (Pre- or post-launch acquisition)	Blended dual-mode updates GPS (Pre- or post-launch acquisition)
Range	15,000–40,000 ft	15,000–100,000+ ft	9,000–80,000 ft	15,000–120,000+ ft
Accuracy	Laser<10m	Laser<<10m	GPS 10m Laser<10m	GPS 10m Laser<<10m
Target Type	Soft Hard Fixed Mobile Moving Target-of-opportunity	Soft Hard, very hard Fixed Mobile Moving Target-of-opportunity	Soft Hard Fixed Mobile Moving Target-of-opportunity	Soft Hard, very hard Fixed Mobile Moving Target-of-opportunity
Impact Control	None	Angle-of-attack Impact angle	Angle-of-attack Impact angle Impact heading	Angle-of-attack
Release Type	Level Dive Loft Toss	Level Dive Loft Toss	Level Dive Loft Toss	Level Dive Loft Toss
Flight Profile	Ballistic	Shaped trajectory	Optimized GPS trajectory	Optimized GPS trajectory
Weather Requirements	Clear	Clear	All weather	All weather
Navigation	Bang-bang	Proportional navigation	Optimized bang-bang	Proportional navigation
Aircraft Electrical Interface Requirements	None	None	1760/1553: Full interface Partial 1553: Minimal interface Power-only interface Enhanced Paveway™ Avionics Kit (EPAK) option provides capability to non-1760 aircraft	1750/1553: Full interface Partial 1553: Minimal interface Power-only interface Enhanced Paveway™ Avionics Kit (EPAK) option provides capability to non-1760 aircraft
Aircraft Electrical Interface Requirements	Limited only by warhead requirements	Limited only by warhead requirements	Limited by warhead requirements plus 1760/1553 interface for full-interface mode	Limited by warhead requirements plus 1760/1553 interface for full-interface mode
Number Produced	More than 200,000	More than 27,000	More than 1,700	More than 1,600
Aircraft Certified	A-4, A-6, A-7, B-52, F-4, F-5 F-14, F-15E, F-16, F/A-18, F-111 F-117, AMX, Buccaneer, Harrier, Hawk, Jaguar, Mirage 2000, Mirage III, Mirage F-1, Super Etendard, Tornado	B-1, B-52, F-14, F-15E, F-16, F/A-18, F-111, F-117, Harrier, Mirage 2000, Mirage F-1, Tornado	Harrier, Mirage, Tornado Undergoing certification on F-15E, F-16 F/A-18, AMX, Super Etendard	B-2, F-14, F-15, F-16, F/A-18, F-117 Tornado Raytheon Company

Courtesy Raytheon

November 1983, followed by the infrared version fourteen months later. In April 1999, the USAF approved further advancement of the GBU-15 with testing conducted at Eglin Air Force Base. The resulting EGBU-15, like the EGBU-12, allows for all-weather, GPS-guided capability with the option of maintaining both infrared and electro-optical guidance greatly improving the weapons versatility.

Developing the EGBU-15 required modifications, not only to the base package, but to the launch aircraft as well. To speed up the compliance process as well as lower development costs, the modification was made in two separate phases. Phase I weapons modification resulted in a $7 million development cost while Phase II cockpit modifications reached $53.5 million. The two phases resulted in a successful weapons modification in record time. It was under budget and saved the taxpayer an average of $200 million compared to similar programs. Reduced initial costs kept the weapon at a relatively low price of approximately $28,000 per unit.

Sandia National Laboratory recently developed the inertial terrain-aided guidance (ITAG) system designed to replace the conventional guidance system in the EGBU-15. As the name indicates, ITAG communicates with an internal radar altimeter in combination with preprogrammed terrain elevation maps to negotiate the immediate terrain regardless of weather conditions, day or night. Target accuracy in the most adverse conditions has resulted in a three-meter circular error probability.

Stepping up in size, the 5,000-pound GBU-28 Bunker Buster consists of a 4,400-pound, penetrating warhead in combination with a laser designator precision guidance package. At the time of the GBU-28's inception, the 2,000-pound GBU-24 was the largest penetrating bomb in USAF inventory capable of being dropped from a fast attack aircraft. Unfortunately, the GBU-24 still was not large enough to destroy some underground targets during Operation Desert Storm. In a period of twenty-eight days beginning on February 1, 1991, the GBU-28 was designed, constructed, tested, and used in combat.

Working around the clock, "bomb specialists" create munitions that are dropped by the F-16C Fighting Falcon and F-15E Strike Eagle aircraft. These munitions specialists build GBU-12 500-pound, laser-guided bombs for missions in Afghanistan. *USAF*

A Lakenheath Strike Eagle drops a 5,000 pound, laser-guided GBU-28 Bunker Buster bomb over the Utah Test and Training Range during a weapons evaluation test. The bomb itself is a 4,400-pound warhead encapsulated within a 600-pound casing. It includes the laser designator guidance package. *USAF*

Contributing to the incredible production speed was the fact that the bomb's housing was created from modified 8-inch, army artillery tubes fitted with LGB kits from a GBU-27. A similar practice was used to construct the GBU-24 by using discarded 8-inch howitzer barrels.

Following Operation Desert Storm, the USAF invested additional funding for further testing. On April 28, 1999, an F-15E Strike Eagle of the 494th Fighter Squadron from Aviano AB, Italy, dropped a GBU-28 against targets in Yugoslavia, making it the first time this weapon was used by an F-15E.

Further tests utilizing an F-15E were conducted as part of the USAF Hardened Target Munitions

program whereby the GBU-28 was to penetrate rock. As a result, an analysis of alternatives was created to determine the best use of future weapons in the 5,000-pound class. An offshoot study known as the Hard and Deeply Buried Target Defeat System used results to create better underground facilities and materials for U.S. and allied forces should a similarly sized weapon become employed by enemy forces.

Best known as the small diameter bomb (SDB), the six-foot, 285-pound bomb contains sixty pounds of explosive and can penetrate more than six feet of reinforced concrete. Having the same penetration capabilities as the larger BLU-109, the small size of the SDB allows for more kills per mission carried out by

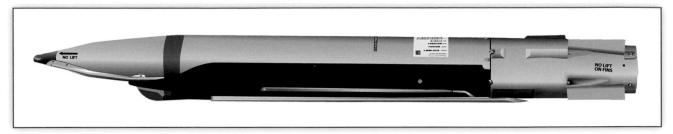

GBU-39 *Courtesy Raytheon*

both manned and unmanned aircraft. Additionally, the smaller size can be credited with less collateral damage to surrounding, non-targeted facilities. The GBU-39 variant of the SDB, the small smart bomb, can destroy either fixed or stationary targets due to its INS/GPS guidance kit. Having a standoff range of more than sixty miles, the GBU-39 utilizes a differential GPS system to initiate constant corrections to its trajectory in all-weather conditions as well as employing an antijam system for greater accuracy.

Although almost all USAF inventory strike aircraft can carry the weapon, it was first developed for use by the F-15E with follow-on integration programs designed for additional platforms. Future use of the SDB in initial attack aircraft like the F-22 will increase target strikes per mission four-fold. It was this very idea that led to its creation by Eglin Air Force Base's Air Force Research Laboratory Munitions Directorate and the goal of increasing aircraft loadout. So successful were the tests, Air Force Chief of Staff, Gen. John P. Jumper, requested it be ready and available for combat by the end of 2006.

CLUSTER BOMB UNITS (CBU)

Munitions under the classification of a cluster bomb are typically intended for destruction of soft targets such as lightly armored vehicles, runways or enemy personnel. They can also be used for dispersal of land mines or even political leaflets. A CBU consists of a hollow shell containing submunitions numbering from as little as three to sometimes thousands of individual devices. These submunitions can either be deployed by the CBU after being released by the aircraft, or the shell of the CBU can remain fixed to the aircraft with subminitions being dispensed over a larger radius. Many variations of CBUs exist today, though most are considered multi-purpose weapons containing various forms of anti-armor, anti-personnel and anti-material submunitions:

- Anti-personnel variants use explosive fragmentation bomblets designed to combat against soft targets such as enemy personnel and unarmored vehicles.
- Anti-tank munitions consist of explosively formed penetrators or shaped charged warheads to pierce heavily armored vehicles.
- Incendiary CBUs are also known as firebombs, as they are intended to do just that. Their purpose is to disperse napalm or submunitions containing white phosphorous.
- Occasionally utilizing a two-stage penetrating submunitions warhead, the anti-runway CBU is designed to dig deep within the runway surface prior to detonation. This enables the weapon to make enormous craters in the runway's surface, rendering it unusable.
- Mine-laying CBUs have been greatly modified by U.S. forces to insure easy cleanup of dispersed mines after an attack. Unlike other CBUs, the mine submunitions remain intact detonating upon contact with a tank, personnel carrier, or enemy personnel. If not detonated within 48 hours of being dispensed, the mines will self-detonate reducing collateral damage.
- Anti-electrical CBUs are designed to disrupt and potentially damage electrical systems by short-circuiting high-voltage power lines. Containing reels of conductive carbon fiber or aluminum-coated glass fiber, the strands spread out above electrical substations shorting out everything they come in contact with.
- Banned by the Chemical Weapons Convention of 1993, chemical dispensing CBUs are no longer

used by the United States or Russia and are currently being disassembled.

- Leaflet dispensing CBUs like the LBU-30 disperse propaganda messages that help sway enemy forces, hopefully reducing the chance of conflict and increased loss of life. Using recycled CBUs, leaflets are packed into the bomblets for a more accurate release resulting in less wind dispersion.

Containing more than seven hundred BLU-77 bomblets, the CBU-59 Anti-Personnel-Anti-Material (APAM) Rockeye II began development in the mid-1970s. Weighing approximately 750 pounds, the 7.5-foot-long CBU-59 can be dropped from as low as 400 feet at speeds of up to Mach 1.3.

Similar to the Rockeye II, the CBU-52 dispenses 220 softball-sized submunitions also designed to destroy minimally armored targets. Each bomblet weights 2.7 pounds and contains 0.65 pounds of explosive dispensed by the activation of multiple variations of proximity fuzes or the MK-339 mechanical timed fuze. The weapon in its entirety weighs in at 766 pounds with a length of about 7.5 feet.

Aircrew preflight an F-15 to check four GBU-39s attached to the undercarriage centerline hardpoints. Also known as the small smart bomb, the GBU-39 contains an inertial guidance kit enabling it to maintain a standoff range of more than sixty miles in all-weather conditions. *USAF*

The CBU-58 contains 650 incendiary bomblets, each with a diameter equal to that of a baseball consisting of 5-gram titanium pellets. Intended to be dispersed over a larger area than the CBU-52, the CBU-58 is only forty pounds heavier. Like the CBU-58, the CBU-71/B carries the same number of bomblets but instead relies on a random delay fuze.

To ease production, the CBU-52, 58, and 71 use the same SUU-30 dispenser to deploy the various bomblets. The dispenser is divided into two halves containing the bomblets with four aluminum fins attached to the rear at ninety-degree angles. Once the fuze is activated a booster ignites and unlocks the forward portion of the dispenser. The two halves are forced apart by ram air dispensing the bomblets.

Containing 202 bomblets designed to destroy armor, personnel, strategic sites, and vehicles, the CBU-87/B Combined Effects Munitions is an all-purpose cluster bomb in the 1,000-pound class. The variations of bomblets contained within the housing include anti-armor, anti-personnel, and incendiary components designed to cover an area of 800 by 400 feet. The collection of bomblets is enclosed in an SW-65 Tactical Munitions Dispenser and can be equipped with a FZU-39 proximity sensor.

In May 1974, the USAF awarded Aerojet the contract to develop what would become the Combined Effects Munitions bomblet. After nearly ten years of development, Aerojet was finally given the go-ahead for initial production with Honeywell (which later became Alliant) being awarded a second-source contract to improve the competitive bidding process. The weapon proved most successful during Operation Desert Storm, with 10,035 CBU-87s being used by the USAF and about 1,000 more deployed by allied forces.

This is a close-up view of Mark 5 bombs and the LANTIRN pod on an F-15E Strike Eagle. The revolutionary LANTIRN system permits the Eagle driver to fly in all-weather conditions, day or night, and allows the aircraft to fly "map-of-the-terrain" with no input from the pilot. *USAF*

Utilizing the same basic SUU-64/B TMD canister as the CBU-87, the CBU-89 GATOR mine is used to dispense larger anti-tank and anti-personnel mines. Also using the same FZU-39 fuze, the CBU-89 deploys a total of ninety-four bomblets with seventy-two of those being anti-tank and twenty-two, anti-personnel. Once deployed, the mines detonate through either target detection, direct contact, decreased battery voltage, or a self-destruct time-out feature that is set prior to aircraft departure. The two forms of mines are triggered by either a tripwire for anti-personnel purposes or by use of a magnetic influence fuze to detect armored vehicles.

Detonation of the CBU-89 can be modified based on the desired minefield area. Using an electromechanical fuze or a proximity sensor, the canister dispenses the mines at varying altitudes modifying the size of the minefield. The higher the altitude, the larger the dispersion of mines.

While most CBUs are designed for medium to low-altitude delivery, high-altitude CBUs utilize a tail kit enabling them to remain on target through inertial guidance correcting for variations in wind direction. These wind corrected munition dispensers (WCMD), or "wick-mid" units, consist of the CBU-103, 104, 105, and 107. Adaptation of a WCMD kit essentially converts a dumb bomb into an accurate smart bomb with an accuracy of approximately thirty feet.

Lockheed Martin was awarded a $21 million contract in January 1997 to begin production of the WCMD to modify nearly 40,000 Tactical Munitions Dispensers. Although DoD officials estimated each unit costing $25,000, a no-nonsense acquisition strategy developed by the Eglin Air Force Base development team reduced unit cost to $8,937. Inclusion of these kits on existing CBUs enable multiple kills per mission, use in adverse weather conditions, improved accuracy and the ability to modify existing canisters for future submunitions according to the Strategic Attack-Air Interdiction Mission Area Plan. An extended-range version (WCMD-ER) incorporates GPS into the kits to further expand the weapons use.

LANTIRN

Though by itself not a weapon, the low-altitude navigation and targeting infrared for night (LANTIRN) pod is an externally mounted device used for low-altitude, nighttime missions even in adverse weather conditions. Technically known as the AN/AAQ-13 navigation pod, the unit's technology enables the aircraft to maintain a preselected altitude negotiating terrain and avoiding obstacles at low levels. The pod provides visual cues by displaying the terrain on a heads-up display via a high-resolution, wide-field, forward-looking infrared navigation system.

Research and development began in 1980 as a means of properly equipping the F-15E and F-16C/D fighters for ground attack capability. A contract for development was awarded to Martin Marietta Corp. whereby testing and evaluation was completed in 1984. Following low rate production, further testing, and eventually full production, the first production LANTIRN was delivered to the USAF on March 31, 1987.

In addition to visual terrain cues, the AN/AAQ-13 also provides an accurate laser designator-rangefinder to increase the accuracy of laser-guided weaponry as well as a missile boresight correlator for use with AGM-65 Maverick missile systems. To ease weapons integration, the LANTIRN system utilizes the information acquired during a mission and upon detection of enemy sites, transfers the target to the missile for launch acquisition. The pod even enables accurate laser measurements for more precise dumb bomb hit accuracy. Easing pilot workload, the AN/AAQ-13 assists the pilot with target recognition and detection enabling the warfighter to better select the appropriate weapon for maximum success.

So popular was the LANTIRN technology, it was soon adapted to the older F-14 Tomcat utilizing and internal GPS/INS, and dubbed the AN/AAQ-14 targeting pod. Use of the pod enabled the USN to retire the venerable A-6 Intruder and enable the F-14 to assume the aircraft's ground-attack role, nicknaming itself the Bombcat.

Langley's 1st Tactical Fighter Wing adorned their Eagle tails with the letters FF for "First Fighter" when they received their F-15s more than thirty years ago. The 1st Tactical Fighter Wing also received the first active-duty F-22 Raptors intended to replace the aging Eagle. *Tyson V. Rininger*

CHAPTER SIX

FUTURE OF THE F-15

THE F-15 HADN'T EVEN CELEBRATED ITS tenth anniversary when the USAF decided to begin the process of finding a replacement. Despite all the new technology the F-15C/D possessed, stealth technology was the new thing and the F-15 simply didn't have it. Additionally, by the time a replacement would enter active service, the F-15 fleet would undoubtedly be facing problems with parts obsolescence and airframes reaching their thirty-year point.

For nearly thirty years, the F-117 flew in missions around the world, including Panama and the Middle East. Stealth technology used by the single-seat fighter

As the F-15 was entering service, so was the top-secret F-117 Nighthawk stealth fighter. Off-the-shelf components were used to maintain secrecy in creating the black jet. The Eagle provided a great deal of the instrumentation as well as the front landing gear and nose assembly. *Tyson V. Rininger*

as well as the B-2 Spirit bomber was so successful, integration into the next generation fighter was a must. Ironically, the F-117 stealth fighter was secretly being built by Lockheed's Skunkworks program utilizing off the shelf components. Of those components, the front landing gear assembly was that of the Eagle's.

By 1986, the USAF had finalized their mission element need statement and awarded two teams $691 million each to develop the advanced tactical fighter. Northrop and McDonnell Douglas teamed up to present the exotic YF-23, while Lockheed, Boeing, and General Dynamics introduced the more practical YF-22. Unlike previous defense contract competitions, the battle between the two aircraft was made very public and like a boxing match, each team gained devoted fans.

Both aircraft were about ten percent larger than the F-15 yet carried twice the amount of internal fuel due to the fifty percent larger wing area. Unfortunately the larger wing area and extra fuel added thirty percent to the combat weight, but the aircraft was

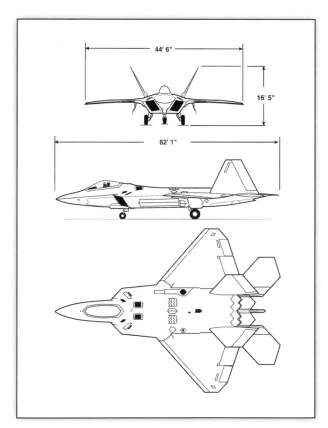

USAF

still capable of performing long-range air superiority missions enabling it to fly deep into enemy territory. Undoubtedly, most chose the YF-23 as their aircraft of choice due to the sleek lines and unique look though it was the YF-22 that ultimately won the competition in April 1991.

The Raptor contains the largest percentage of composite materials included on any fighter built thus far. Containing thirty-nine percent titanium for areas in need of reinforcement, twenty-four percent of the aircraft is made of composite materials with sixteen percent being aluminum and one percent thermoplastic. The fuselage frame, doors, intermediate wing spars, and skin panels consisting of honeycomb sandwich design are all composed of carbon fiber material.

The F/A-22 Raptor is equipped with the AN/APG-77 radar developed by Northrop Grumman and Raytheon Electronic Systems using an active electronically scanned antennae array of 2,000 transmitter-receiver modules. This particular setup allows for improved agility with a low radar cross-section and wide bandwidth.

Powered by two P&W F119-100 engines, the revolutionary powerplant is a low-bypass afterburning turbofan equipped with lightweight, wide chord, hollow fan blades. Engine exhaust is cooled slightly by flowing over heat-absorbing ceramic tiles built in to the Hamilton Standard controlled dual redundant full authority digital engine control. This entire process not only enables the aircraft to cruise at supersonic speeds without afterburner (Mach 1.5 as demonstrated), but utilize the thrust vectoring system for enhanced maneuverability.

Inside the cockpit, the F/A-22 took cues from the F-15's elementary design by incorporating a revised HOTAS control. Presented to the pilot are six color LCDs that display the air and ground tactical situation including threat priority, identity, and tracking information as well as communication, navigation, identification, and flight information. In addition, the secondary displays show ground threats, stores management, and other threat information. Above the panel lies the HUD that displays flight control information as well as target status, weapon status, shoot cues, and the various weapons envelopes.

Internally, the Raptor can carry an assortment of AIM-9M or AIM-9X missiles along with the

Presented to the public in November 1990, the advanced tactical fighter YF-22 prototype sits proudly in front of an American Flag. The fuselage, stabilizers, and other elements were smoothed and rounded over the course of its ten-year development before active duty. *USAF*

short-range Sidewinder and the new AIM-120A, AMRAAM, and a number of 1,000-pound GBU-32 JDAMs. Above the left intake resides an internally mounted M61A2 Vulcan cannon capable of firing 480 rounds of 20mm ammunition at approximately 100 rounds per second. Though rarely used, the Raptor also has four external hardpoints on the wings that can carry additional AIM-120s or external fuel tanks.

Upon completion of the milestone II review in 1991, the USAF announced plans to procure 648 F/A-22 Raptor airframes at a cost of $86.6 billion.

Later that year, two contracts were awarded for EMD of the F/A-22 and the P&W F119 engine for a total of $10.9 billion.

Following a bottom-up review conducted by the DoD in September 1993, the number of airframes was reduced to 442 with an estimated cost of $71.6 billion. Regardless, assembly of the first flyable airframe began in Kent, Washington, on December 8, 1993.

Of course, not everyone was a fan of the new aircraft. In a report dated March 25, 1994, to the Chairman, Legislation and National Security Subcommittee,

YF-23

Ten years after the F-15 was placed into active service, Soviet Fighters once again posed a threat to U.S. aerial dominance. Aircraft like the Migoyan MiG-29 Fulcrum and Sukhoi's Su-27 Flanker showed incredible agility and phenomenal performance. Even though the United States had secretly developed the F-117 Night Hawk stealth fighter, the Soviets were also demonstrating stealthy characteristics within their airframe designs.

In 1981, the USAF took action by initiating a Mission Element Need Statement for a new airframe that would not only embody the stealthy characteristics of the F-117 and the Northrop B-2 Spirit, but also incorporate attributes worthy of maintaining the F-15's air superiority. Features such as supersonic cruise, extreme maneuverability and internal weapons storage were just some of the requirements listed for the advanced tactical fighter (ATF) program. It was expected that the winner of the ATF program would also go toward the replacement of the F-14 Tomcat, NATF, but due to funding, the USN portion of the program was dropped in 1990.

Two teams were awarded a $691 million fixed contract in October 1986 to create this new fighter. Northrop/McDonnell Douglas presented the sleek YF-23 and the Lockheed/Boeing/General Dynamics team unveiled the slightly edgier YF-22. While the YF-22 didn't receive the name Raptor until just prior to entering service, the YF-23 team chose to call their aircraft the Black Widow II. The gray version of the YF-23 was affectionately known as the "Gray Ghost," though technically they were both referred to as PAV-1 and PAV-2. Both the YF-22 and YF-23 took advantage of newer technologies including lighter-weight alloys, more powerful propulsion systems, increased use of composite materials, and integration of advanced flight control systems.

The YF-23 featured a diamond-shaped wing design with a pair of well-spaced engines and an off-the-shelf, forward cockpit and nose wheel assembly from the newly activated F-15E. In the rear, the elevators and stabilizer were combined to create a highly angled, single-control surface known as a "ruddervator." The aircraft managed to achieve a sustained supersonic speed without the use of afterburner and achieved a top speed of Mach 1.8 during development testing at Edwards Air Force Base. Since the YF-23 was slightly more aerodynamic than the YF-22, its cruising speed excelled with the YF-23 averaging Mach 1.25 and the YF-22 at Mach 1.17.

To maintain stealth characteristics, airframe design incorporated the lessons learned from the B-2 program, evident by the beavertail trailing edge, along with use of radar absorbent material (RAM). Heat from the exhaust was cooled via rear jet nozzle troughs containing heat-absorbing tiles. Reducing the heat

signature of the aircraft makes it a more difficult target for infrared and heat-seeking missiles as well as less detectable for ground-based radar systems. Two P&W F119 engines powered PAV-1 while PAV-2 contained two General Electric F120 engines. Although the YF-22 team chose to use heat-absorbing tiles as well, they incorporated thrust-vectoring nozzles improving low-speed agility as compared to the YF-23 team's primary focus on stealthness and supercruise technology.

The YF-23 enhanced the stealth characteristics with a technique known as blending. Beginning at the nose of the aircraft, a small chine runs the length of the forward canopy section eventually blending with the wing. Not only does this provide improved aerodynamics, but practically eliminates drag-causing vortices and adds to the structural rigidity of the airframe. The aircraft presents a lower radar cross section with blending, in contrast to the design of the F-117. The F-117 achieved the same effect by avoiding certain angles that would allow radar signals to bounce off the aircraft, but sacrificed aerodynamics and overall speed in the process.

Other advancements introduced by the YF-23 included the wing-blended nacelles containing the engines. The larger fuselage enabled the engines to be spaced further apart and provided greater internal weapons storage. Engine airflow intakes took on a new look with an upward angled inlet allowing radar waves to be reflected and dissipated before hitting the rough-edged and fast-moving blades of the engine's compressor face. The larger wing design created greater fuel capacity and longer range with fewer aerial refueling requirements.

The general public and many of those on the ATF advisory team found the YF-23 more aesthetically pleasing than the Y-22, but those looks made it a very unstable platform. Incorporating a fly-by-wire control system, developed and utilized first by the General Dynamics F-16 Fighting Falcon, the Y-23 was certainly agile. The YF-22 still managed to win the ATF competition.

The YF-22 demonstrated a greater ease of maintainability, lower cost, and greater versatility for future development. With Secretary of the Air Force Donald B. Rice at the helm, the contract went to Lockheed and its subcontractors in April 1991 to further develop what would be initially known as the F/A-22 Raptor. Just prior to entering active duty, the attack portion of the program was dropped and the Raptor became known simply as the F-22.

Both PAV-1 and PAV-2 prototypes were turned over to the NASA Dryden Research Facility at Edwards Air Force Base following the ATF program trials. NASA briefly used one of the airframes for a calibration technique study, though NASA never intended to fly either aircraft. Currently PAV-2 (S/N 87-801) is on display at the Western Museum of Flight in Hawthorne, California, and PAV-1 (S/N 87-800) was recently moved to the National Museum of the USAF in Dayton, Ohio.

GENERAL CHARACTERISTICS
- Crew: 1 (pilot)
- Length: 67 feet 5 inches (20.60 meters)
- Wingspan: 43 feet 7 inches (13.30 meters)
- Height: 13 feet 11 inches (4.30 meters)
- Wing area: 900 feet² (88 meters²)
- Empty weight: 29,000 pounds (14,970 kilograms)
- Loaded weight: 51,320 pounds (23,327 kilograms)
- Max takeoff weight: 62,000 pounds (29,029 kilograms)
- Powerplant: General Electric YF120 or Pratt & Whitney YF119, 35,000 pounds per foot (156 kilograms per Newton) each

PERFORMANCE
- Maximum speed: Mach 2.2+ (1,650+ miles per hour, 2,655+ kilometers per hour) at altitude
- Cruise speed: Mach 1.6+ est. (1,060+ miles per hour, 1,706+ kilometers per hour) supercruise at altitude
- Combat radius: 865–920 miles [8] (750–800 nautical miles, 1,380–1480 kilometers)
- Service ceiling 65,000 feet (19,800 meters)
- Wing loading: 54 pounds per foot² (265 kilogram per meter²)
- Thrust/weight: 1.36

ARMAMENT
None as tested but provisions made for
- 120mm M61 Vulcan cannon
- 4 air-to-air missiles, AIM-120 AMRAAM, and AIM-9 Sidewinder

The YF-23 was in many cases a superior design to the F-22 Raptor, however overall practicality made the Raptor a more efficient and less costly aircraft, according to the joint manufacturing entities. Despite the F-22 winning the overall competition, stealth technology and development reached new levels due to the fierce competition to be the next air superiority fighter. *NASA*

Committee on Government Operations, and the House of Representatives, the thought of replacing the F-15 at that time was believed to be premature and unwarranted. The following report was made with the support of the National Security and International Affairs Division due to concerns of unrealistic budgeting and increasing cost:

The Honorable John Conyers, Jr.
Chairman, Legislation and National Security
    Subcommittee
Committee on Government Operations
House of Representatives

Dear Mr. Chairman:

In December 1993, we issued to the House and Senate Committees on Armed Services and the Subcommittees on Defense, Committees on Appropriations, a classified report on the F-22 as the planned replacement for the F-15. As you subsequently requested, this is an unclassified version of that report. The report presents the results of the first of a series of reviews we plan to conduct on the F-22 program. We currently have underway a review of the program's development progress and a review of the management of F-22 software development.

The development and production of F-22 air superiority fighters is estimated to cost $99.1 billion (then-year dollars). The F-22, with operational capability planned for 2003, is designed to replace the Air Force's F-15 air superiority fighter, which began operations in the mid-1970s. To ascertain why the F-22 was needed to replace the F-15, we have evaluated information provided by the Department of Defense (DOD) describing performance characteristics of foreign weapon systems that may be encountered in air-to-air combat, and compared it with features of the F-15 weapon system. Considering the huge investments required for tactical aviation modernization programs, we also evaluated whether the F-22, as designed, had the potential for joint use among the services and for use in multiple missions, which are being emphasized by the Under Secretary of Defense for Acquisition (Statement on Tactical Aviation by the Under Secretary of Defense for Acquisition, to the Defense Subcommittee of the Senate Appropriations Committee, May 12, 1993).

The P&W F119 engine is capable of producing 35,000 pounds of thrust. This photograph shows it in full afterburner during an engine test inside the Hush House on Tyndall Air Force Base, Florida. The engine's immense power can turn an aircraft on a dime at practically zero airspeed, while remaining in complete control of basic flight. *USAF*

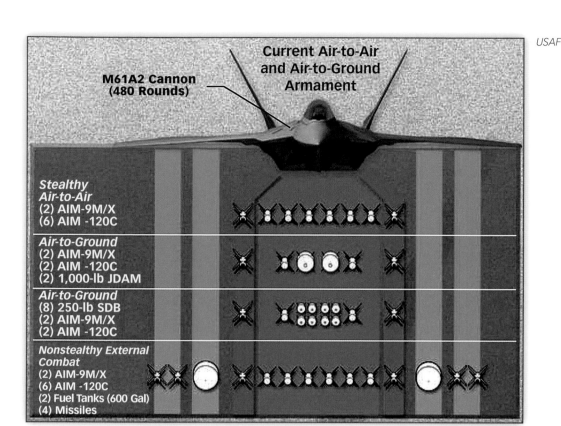

M61A2 Cannon
(480 Rounds)

Current Air-to-Air
and Air-to-Ground
Armament

Stealthy
Air-to-Air
(2) AIM-9M/X
(6) AIM -120C

Air-to-Ground
(2) AIM-9M/X
(2) AIM -120C
(2) 1,000-lb JDAM

Air-to-Ground
(8) 250-lb SDB
(2) AIM-9M/X
(2) AIM -120C

Nonstealthy External
Combat
(2) AIM-9M/X
(6) AIM -120C
(2) Fuel Tanks (600 Gal)
(4) Missiles

Appendix I contains our review's scope and methodology.

RESULTS IN BRIEF

The F-22 program was initiated in 1981 to meet the evolving threat in the mid-1990s. This threat revolved around a fighter threat that had a significant quantitative advantage and was becoming more capable with the introduction of two new high performance fighters.

Since the F-22 program entered full-scale development in 1991, the severity of the projected military threat in terms of quantities and capabilities has declined. Instead of confronting thousands of modern Soviet fighters, U.S. air forces are expected to confront potential adversary air forces that include few fighters that have the capability to challenge the F-15—the U.S. front line fighter. Our analysis shows that the F-15 exceeds the most advanced threat system expected to exist. We assumed no improvements will

be made to the F-15 but the capability of the "most advanced threat" assumes certain modifications. Further, our analysis indicates that the current inventory of F-15s can be economically maintained in a structurally sound condition until 2015 or later.

Thus, the F-22's initial operational capability can be delayed 7 years and its planned production start date of 1996 can be postponed to a future date deemed appropriate by DOD to meet the new initial operational capability date.

In addition to a declining need for the F-22 to counter threats, the aircraft has not been designed to emphasize multiple missions or joint use among the services, important features for future solutions for tactical aircraft modernization, according to the Under Secretary of Defense for Acquisition. The F-22, as designed, will be a land-based fighter, not capable of operating from Navy aircraft carriers. Further, the F-22 is principally

Hughes Aircraft Company employee Steve DeLeon looks into the world's most advanced high-speed computer system for use onboard a fighter aircraft. Hughes delivered the F-22's first common integrated processor in 2008. Acting as the aircraft's brain, the common integrated processor hosts and executes software for the avionics systems. *USAF*

designed to perform one mission—air superiority against opposing fighters.

BACKGROUND

Air superiority means dominating the air battle to the extent that friendly air and surface forces can conduct operations without prohibitive interference by enemy air forces. During the Persian Gulf War, coalition air forces achieved air superiority during the first few hours. Only 33 air-to-air encounters occurred between U.S. and adversary

fighters. F-15s were involved in 31 of these 33 encounters and succeeded in each one.

The F-22 is one of several planned Air Force and Navy aircraft production programs associated with the tactical aircraft modernization program. DOD approved the initiation of F-22 engineering and manufacturing development in 1991 and the start of production is planned for January 1996 with the purchase of long lead production materials. The Air Force plans to take delivery of the first 5 production aircraft in 1999 and an additional 80 by the time the aircraft achieves initial operational capability in 2003.

THE PROJECTED FIGHTER THREAT LESS FORMIDABLE THAN PREVIOUSLY PROJECTED

The break up of the Warsaw Pact and the Soviet Union lessened the quantity and the quality of the projected fighter threat. For example, in 1993, DOD identified seven countries that typify the fighter forces that pose a threat to the United States. Except for China, these countries have fighter forces that range from a low of 188 to a high of 460 aircraft. And all seven countries currently have only a few high-performance fighters that come close to matching the F-15's performance capabilities.

In contrast, the U.S. Air Force has about 900 F-15s. Because the foreign high-performance fighter aircraft are expensive, DOD believes that few purchases of these aircraft will be made in the future.

U.S. AIRCRAFT CHARACTERISTICS EXCEED THE PROJECTED THREAT

Our analysis shows the existing F-15C was superior in four out of five major performance categories against the most likely advanced fighter threat. Further, our analysis assumes no improvements will be made to the F-15s but the capability of the most advanced threat assumes certain

(continued on page 146)

With fewer government threats and sufficient current technology, the F-15 may survive longer than predicted. Furthermore, cost versus performance evaluation of the new F-22 Raptor found the aircraft insufficient and orders for F-22s were cut in half. This forced a number of F-15s to remain in service for many years to come. *Tyson V. Rininger*

NASA F-15 S/MTD

Eagle 71-0290 was one of the initial F-15s assigned to Edwards Air Force Base for test and development purposes. Originally dubbed TF-1 and first flown on July 7, 1973, the two-seater was responsible for stability, control, and performance testing. As development continued, it was renamed TF-15A, and finally F-15B #1. Little did anyone know how pivotal this airframe would become in the advancements of airframe and thrust dynamics.

Exercises originally conducted by McDonnell Douglas called for the F-15B to be highly modified with integrated foreplanes up front, resembling abnormally large moveable canards, and vectored thrust nozzles in the rear. The Eagle was called the short takeoff and landing/maneuver technology demonstrator (STOL/MTD). The goal was to perform better at low speeds and land in short distances on bomb-damaged runways. With the combination of the canard's improved agility, derived from an F/A-18 stabilator, and the twenty-degree deflection of the jet nozzles, the F-15 demonstrated take-off speeds of as little as 42 miles per hour. Additionally, the STOL/MTD could decelerate rapidly with thrust reversal and land in just 1,650 feet of runway compared to the required 7,500 for a base F-15. It also used twenty-five percent less runway on take-off.

In 1993, the aircraft was loaned to NASA for further research. The standard F100 engines were replaced with the more powerful F100-229 variant and the thrust nozzles were improved by adding pitch and yaw movements. Studies obtained by the vectored-thrust technology were later incorporated into the newer, F-22 Raptor.

Between 1993 and 1998, NASA flew the improved aircraft testing the limitations of flight, calling it the F-15 ACTIVE (advanced control technology for integrated vehicles). Combining the improved aerodynamics, flight surfaces, and vectored thrust technology enabled the aircraft to be the first to achieve supersonic yaw-vectoring as well as the first to use pitch and yaw thrust at speeds of up to Mach 2.

The Eagle became known as the F-15 IFCS in 1999. The Intelligent Flight Control System (IFCS) was developed to maximize the aircraft's capabilities and performance as well as provide improved safety for the flight crew. NASA wanted a flight control system that allowed the aircraft to fly in conditions normally considered unrecoverable. This technology was a joint venture involving the NASA Dryden Flight Research Center, NASA Ames Research Center, Boeing Phantom Works, the Georgia Institute of Technology, and the Institute for Scientific Research at West Virginia.

The first F-15B, originally dubbed TF-1, has been converted to a STOL aircraft utilizing F/A-18 stabilators as canards and thrust vectored nozzles for propulsion. The NASA aircraft was known as the S/MTD, or short takeoff and landing/maneuver technology demonstrator. *NASA*

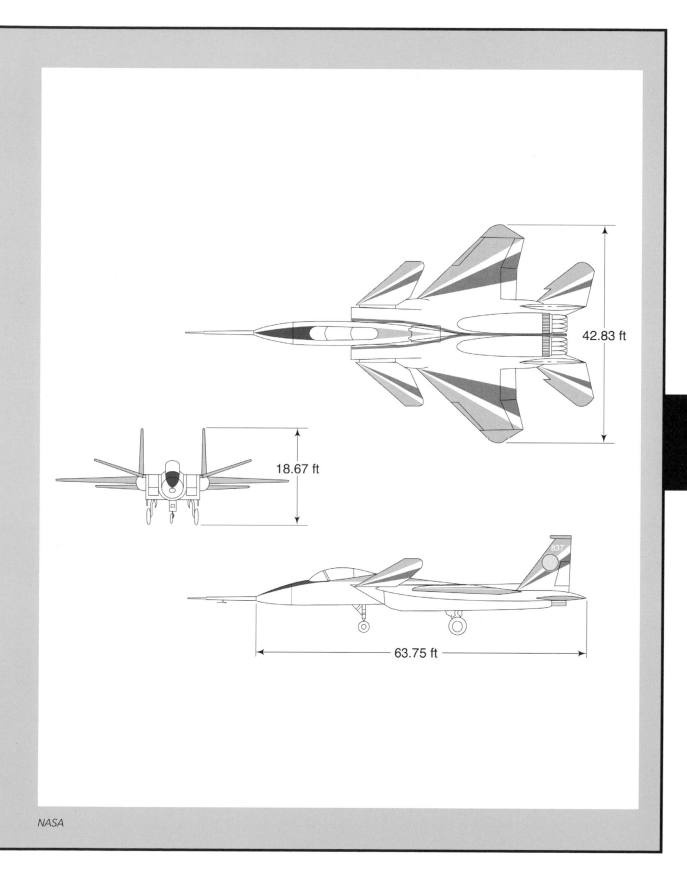

42.83 ft

18.67 ft

63.75 ft

837

NASA

The F-15 IFCS incorporated a self-learning neural network that has the ability to train itself based on the aircraft's ever-changing flight characteristics. This technology assists both military and civilian aircraft in achieving the best performance along with preventing crashes when an aircraft could otherwise have been saved. Inputs to the central computer are gathered via thirty-one separate readings from roll, pitch, and yaw axes as well as the various control surfaces themselves.

F-15B "QUIET SPIKE"

Gulfstream Aerospace and NASA's Dryden Flight Research Center tested the structural integrity of the telescopic "Quiet Spike" sonic boom mitigator on a NASA F-15B test bed aircraft. The Quiet Spike was developed as a means of controlling and reducing the sonic boom caused by an aircraft "breaking" the sound barrier.

Made of advanced composite materials, the Quiet Spike weighed some 470 pounds and extended from 14 feet in subsonic flight, to 24 feet in supersonic flight. Gulfstream was awarded a patent for the Quiet Spike in March 2004. The device went through extensive ground testing, including wind-tunnel testing, before it was installed on an F-15B aircraft and flown. The F-15B is capable of flying at speeds in excess of Mach 2.0, or two times the speed of sound.

Once the Quiet Spike proved to be structurally sound, it could be incorporated onto advanced low-boom configuration aircraft to further control and mitigate adverse acoustic impacts of supersonic flight. It was hoped that the Quiet Spike could change the traditional N-wave sonic boom into smooth and more rounded pressure waves, shaped roughly like a sine wave or a sideways "S." This resulting wave shape is a softer sound that is quieter than the Concorde sonic boom by a factor of 10,000.

The spike was first tested supersonically on October 20, 2006, and is actuated by an electric winch-driven cable and pulley system. Project pilot James Smolka flew thirty-two test flights by January 2007, with optimistic test results.

In 1993, the aircraft was again modified and called ACTIVE (advanced control technology for integrated vehicles). Here it is shown in flight over the Mojave Desert near Edwards Air Force Base, California. Note the removal of the vertical thrust vectored nozzles and the use of newer, yaw-vectoring circular nozzles. *NASA*

Gulfstream Aerospace and NASA's Dryden Flight Research Center are testing the structural integrity of a telescopic "Quiet Spike" sonic boom mitigator on the F-15B test bed. The Quiet Spike was developed as a means of controlling and reducing the sonic boom caused by an aircraft breaking the sound barrier. *NASA*

(continued from page 141)

modifications. Our detailed analysis has been classified by DOD.

In addition to having superior aircraft, the U.S. Air Force has other capabilities that enhance its air superiority mission that potential adversaries lack. The E-3 Airborne Warning and Control System is considered by DOD to be the most advanced command and control system in the world, assisting tactical aircraft in locating, identifying, tracking, and attacking enemy aircraft at great distances.

DOD officials also consider U.S. pilot training methods to be far more advanced than any foreign country. U.S. pilots are often trained in advanced combat tactics that are not taught anywhere else.

F-15S ARE EXPECTED TO HAVE SERVICE LIFE UNTIL 2015

DOD cited, as a factor in its 1981 decision to replace the F-15, projected limits on the F-15's structural service life. However,

An F-22 Raptor, assigned to the 422nd Test and Evaluation Squadron, sits ominously on the flight line at Nellis Air Force Base. Major Michael Hernandez, a Raptor pilot, discusses preflight operations with Senior Airman James Douglass, a Raptor Crew Chief. The Raptor is undoubtedly the most complex fighter built to date. *USAF*

Lieutenant Colonel Dirk Smith, Commander, 94th Fighter Squadron, peels away from Maj. Kevin Dolata, Assistant Director of Operations, 94th Fighter Squadron, during the delivery flight of the first F-22A Raptor fighters to Langley. The 94th Fighter Squadron is the second squadron at Langley to receive the new stealth fighter. The 27th Fighter Squadron was the first recipient of the new jet on May 12, 2005. *USAF*

a 1990 DOD evaluation indicated that the F-15s might have a service life longer than originally expected. Since then, testing has demonstrated that the Air Force can further extend the F-15's service life. Based on this recent testing, our analysis shows that none of the 918 F-15s that were in the inventory in July 1992 will begin to exceed their expected economic service lives until 2014.

F-22 AS DESIGNED OFFERS LITTLE VERSATILITY FOR NAVY ROLES OR SURFACE ATTACK MISSIONS

As currently designed, the F-22 will be a highly specialized aircraft to be used by one service—the Air Force—to perform one mission—air superiority. The F-22 program does not appear to meet all the tactical modernization goals set forth by the Under Secretary of Defense for Acquisition. The Under Secretary testified in May 1993 that DOD intended to take full advantage of commonality and jointness in tactical modernization programs, emphasizing both multimission or multi-role platforms and commonality among the services.

During the air war in the Persian Gulf, there was not a need for large numbers of fighters having only the capability to perform air superiority missions. Of the

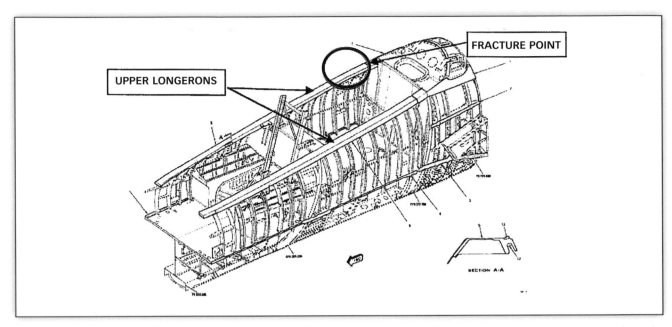

Reports (see "Executive Summary," page 153) found the mishap aircraft break-up was initiated by failure of the right upper longeron, just forward of the CFS 377 bulkhead splice. The upper longerons in the forward fuselage are single load-path structures. Failure of either longeron results in loss of the structural capability to carry the applied loads. Surface fracture analysis by Boeing and AFRL laboratory identified a fatigue crack with multiple origins in the upper web of the MA longeron. The fatigue crack progressed both inboard and outboard through the web. As the crack continued to grow through the inboard flange of the longeron, the crack eventually led to overload failure of the remaining longeron section. *USAF*

215 Iraqi aircraft destroyed or captured, 182 were destroyed on the ground by bombs or were captured by ground troops. Only 33 aircraft, or 15 percent, were destroyed in air-to-air combat. DOD's report to Congress, Conduct of the Persian Gulf War, indicated that few Iraqi aircraft left the ground, in large measure, because U.S. forces quickly destroyed the Iraqi air defense command and control network.

The F-22 is currently designed to operate from land bases only. It cannot operate from Navy carriers or readily be converted for such operations. Although the F-22, like other fighters, has some inherent air-to-ground capability, the F-22 program is not funded to develop that capability. DOD said plans are now being made to initiate development of an air-to-ground capability for the F-22.

The Defense Science Board, in a report on the modernization of tactical aviation forces, stated that in the future, the greater economic constraints and lower rates and quantities of combat aircraft to be acquired will tend to make the use of common aircraft and/or components more attractive than it has been in the past. They recognized that this may require some compromise in mission capabilities. For example, Air Force applications of a common aircraft for land and aircraft carrier use may be heavier than they would be if designed only for land-based operations. We agree with the Board and also believe that the less formidable military threat could make certain compromises acceptable that would not have been acceptable prior to the changes in the projections of the future threat.

The theme that the services need to cooperate was sounded again by a special task force sponsored by the Board to evaluate the fiscal implications of DOD's proposed future years defense plans. The task force noted the need for the services to cooperate in the development of future systems because of future funding shortfalls. It concluded that

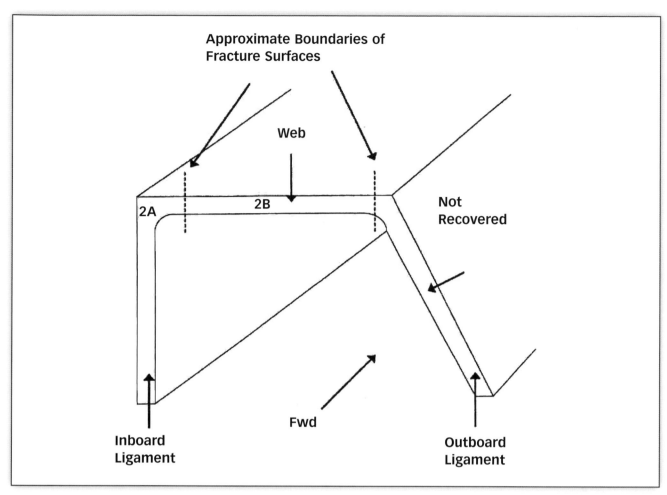

Approximate Boundaries of Fracture Surfaces

Web

2A 2B

Not Recovered

Inboard Ligament

Fwd

Outboard Ligament

This schematic of the right upper longeron, forward of FS 379, shows the relative location of fracture surfaces. Thickness undercut conditions were found within the web portion of the longeron in two separate places. Original blueprint specifications for longeron thickness were not met. The additional strains of the existing crack and the pilot's reaching 7.8 G-tolerance took their toll on the aircraft. *USAF*

the aircraft programs now under development will not all be affordable at the funding levels projected for the rest of this decade.

RECOMMENDATIONS

Because F-15s, by most measures, are more capable than the most likely threat related to the air superiority mission and because F-15s are expected to have service lives extending until 2014, we recommend that the Secretary of Defense defer the initial operational capability of the F-22 7 years and adjust the currently planned production start date accordingly. In addition, because the F-22, as designed, does not incorporate the features of multiservice use and multimission capability being articulated by the Under Secretary of Defense for Acquisition, we also recommend that the Secretary reconsider whether it is appropriate to continue the development of the F-22 as a single-service aircraft designed principally to perform only the air superiority mission.

AGENCY COMMENTS AND OUR EVALUATION

In commenting on a draft of the classified report, DOD disagreed with our recommendations and stated that although there had been substantial changes to the

FOREIGN EAGLES

So successful was the Eagle design, it quickly garnered interest from other countries such as Israel, Saudi Arabia, Korea, and Japan. Soon orders began pouring in for additional aircraft with slightly subdued echnology.

The first allied customer to place an order for the Eagle was the Israeli Air Force in 1975. Israel was in desperate need for new aircraft having lost a total of two hundred airframes of various types following the 1967 Six Day War, the War of Attrition against Syria and Egypt lasting until 1970, and the Yom Kippur war in 1973.

Iran's recent acquisition of the F-14 Tomcat with its longer range prompted Israel to choose the F-15A rather than the F-16A considered earlier. In addition, the F-15's APG-63 provides better radar than the F-16's shorter range APG-65. In 1975, the IAF placed an order for twenty-five F-15A/B aircraft and began receiving them on December 10, 1976, under the program name "Peace Fox." Upon receipt of the F-15I "Baz" (Hebrew for "falcon"), the IAF created the 133rd Squadron especially for the new aircraft and equipped them to carry the Israeli-built Shafrir 2 IR AAM along with Rafael Python 3 advanced IR AAMs.

Besides the incredible air-to-air kill ratio earned by the IAF, they managed to modify the Eagle to successfully carry out ground operations. Although the USAF had successfully tested the F-15 for air-to-ground capability, it determined the bombing aspect of the Eagle should never impede on its primary goal of aerial supremacy.

Following Operation Desert Storm, the United States offered twenty-five additional discounted F-15s to the IAF, under the name Peace Fox V. The Eagles, previously used by various Air National Guard units, had not gone through the MSIP program. The Israeli Strike Eagles arrived in 1992, along with a program to update legacy Eagles by incorporating the AMRAAM missile system along with the helmet mounted cueing system.

To date, the IAF claims a 50-0 kill ratio, more enemy kills from use of the F-15 than American forces.

Partially produced and assembled by Mitsubishi, the F-15J and two-seat F-15DJ is Japan's primary air superiority fighter for the Japanese Air Self Defense Force (JASDF). They were created from indigenously manufactured sub-assemblies and engineered equipment. The F-15J lacks the sensitive ECM and radar warning equipment along with nuclear capability. Mitsubishi also replaced the AN/ALG-135 and AN/ALR-56 RHAWS with the J/ALQ-8 and J/APR-4, respectively.

The first Eagle arrived in Japan on July 15, 1980, under the name "Peace Eagle" with a total of six F-15Js and eight F-15DJs delivered intact or as kits in large subassemblies. The remaining 199 aircraft produced by Mitsubishi gave the JASDF a total force of 213 F-15Js. Japan is now the largest user of Eagles outside the United States.

Known as the Peace Sun, F-15C/D series of Eagles, Saudi Arabia originally intended to operate the F-14 for some of the same reasons as the IAF. The Royal Saudi Air Force wanted both the Tomcat's long range and weapons ability and to combat the Shah of Iran's F-14s should they fall into the wrong hands. Eventually it was determined the F-15S would be the aircraft of choice and by 1982, forty-six F-15Cs and sixteen F-15Ds were delivered in addition to five E-3A AWACS aircraft.

In response to Israeli Air Force concerns regarding the sale of F-15s to Saudi Arabia, the United States placed limitations on the use of Saudi F-15s to only sixty, operating aircraft. This meant two aircraft were to be held in the United States as attrition aircraft and limited use of CFTs. It also denied Saudi Arabia the range necessary to cause conflict with Israel. Meanwhile the IAF has become the most significant user of CFTs on F-15C airframes.

The Saudi Air Force has seen very little action, though they did assist allied forces during Operation Desert Storm. To date, the Saudi Air Force is credited with four kills total, including two Iranian F-4Es and two Iraqi Mirage F1EQs.

Following Boeing's takeover of McDonnell Douglas, the Republic of Korea was offered the advanced F-15K, an updated variant of the F-15E Strike Eagle, in October 2000. Expanding the capabilities of the existing AN/APG-70 radar, the F-15K will make use of the APG-63 (v) 1 as well as have the ability to launch the AGM-130 and JDAM.

Seven years later, the Boeing Company announced Singapore's 2005 order of eight F-15SGs, also a variant of the F-15E. The order was later followed up by an additional four F-15SGs.

world order, DOD is convinced its direction on the F-22 program is correct. Further, DOD did not concur with our characterizations of (1) the threat, (2) current U.S. capability, (3) F-22 capabilities, and (4) its objectives for aircraft modernization.

Our threat information comes from DOD intelligence agencies and we believe it is accurately characterized. Concerning the capabilities of the F-15, DOD merely argues that the F-22 would do a better job than the F-15. We do not necessarily disagree with this, but suggest that a more realistic view would be that the United States does not need the extra air superiority by 2003 as planned, considering the costs involved and the unlikely increase in the threat. Our report is based on a methodology used by DOD for comparative evaluations of the characteristics of fighters, and on discussions with responsible DOD officials. Aircraft characteristics were obtained from defense intelligence organizations and Air Force weapon system program offices. Therefore, we believe the concerns set forth in the DOD comments concerning the characterization of the threat and current U.S. capabilities are unfounded.

We have modified the report to recognize that the F-22 has some inherent air-to-ground capability (like most other fighter aircraft) and that DOD has initiated plans to develop that capability.

The agency comments also indicate that DOD has no policy that requires aircraft to be designed for multiservice use or that requires the same aircraft be used to meet the common needs of the services. However, these comments appear to be at odds with the May 1993 congressional testimony of the Under Secretary of Defense for Acquisition.

We are sending copies of this report to the Secretary of Defense, the Director of the Office of Management and Budget, the original four congressional requesters, and other interested parties. Major contributors to this report are listed in appendix II. Please contact me on (202) xxx-xxxx if you or your staff have any questions concerning this report.

Sincerely yours,

Louis J. Rodrigues
Director, Systems Development and
    Production Issues

SCOPE AND METHODOLOGY
Appendix I

In conducting our work, we visited the Defense Intelligence Agency; the Foreign Aerospace Science and Technology Center; the F-22, F-16, and F-15 System Program Offices; and the Development Planning Directorate at the Air Force's Aeronautical Systems Center (Air Force Materiel Command).

In making aircraft performance comparisons, we examined documents regarding the capabilities of threat aircraft, including the Multicommand Manual 3-1, Threat Reference Guide and Countertactics. Using performance categories and scenarios from this document, which Air Force officials agreed provided pertinent categories for comparison, we requested consistent foreign and U.S. aircraft performance data from the applicable Defense organizations. We received foreign aircraft information from the Air Force's Foreign Aerospace Science and Technology Center (Air Force Intelligence Command), and U.S. aircraft information from the F-14, F-15, F-16, F-18, and F-22 System Program Offices. We compared the F-15C to the most severe threat aircraft projected to be available in substantial quantities to illustrate the capabilities of U.S. fighter aircraft. We did not evaluate the F-15C's capabilities against ground-based threats, such as surface-to-air missiles because the primary need for the F-22, as stated in Selected acquisition Reports, was to counter the emergence of large numbers of advanced Soviet fighters, and because a number of other weapon systems exist for the primary purpose of neutralizing those threats. Similarly, we did not evaluate the capabilities of threat fighter aircraft against U.S. surface-to-air missile systems.

We used this data to perform aircraft capability comparisons involving 5 categories and 32 characteristics identified as most pertinent to the air superiority mission by Air Combat Command. The 32 characteristics are distributed throughout the 5 categories as follows: flight performance (11), radar (3), long-range missiles (8), short-range missiles (8), and combat mission radius (2).

To conclude that one aircraft was better than another in one of the five categories, the aircraft was required to have superior statistics in a majority of the compared characteristics. If two aircraft had equal characteristics, they were determined to be even in that category.

We performed our work from December 1992 through August 1993 in accordance with generally accepted government auditing standards.

Despite the letter's reasoning and justification, budget cuts in fiscal years 1994 and 1995 forced the program to reschedule, resulting in an eleven month delay of the first flight and an eighteen month delay in reaching the Milestone III goal. By fiscal year 1996, a third rephase of the program was needed due to further budget restraints.

A further cut in aircraft numbers was made in May 1997 reducing the 438 desired aircraft to that of 339. The lower quantity also slowed production from 48 airframes per year to 36.

Changes to the overall quantity ordered had drastic effects on the unit price. A single F/A-22 was fetching $300 million each compared to the F-15's $55 million per plane cost. This process would continue as aircraft needs were routinely reevaluated and budget concerns were addressed.

The F-22 was indeed the most complex fighter ever built. Containing more than 15,000 self-diagnostic points in the airframe and engine along with another 15,000 reserved for the avionics, the Raptor insured ease of maintenance and relief on pilot workload. Engineers, maintenance personnel, and pilots were all integral to the F/A-22's development and in the process logical thought was introduced. One resounding point was made during the development process asking why does an aircraft have to be any more complicated than the average automobile. Every switch, button, and knob received scrutiny as to whether it was absolutely necessary to be in the cockpit. This same rational line of thinking was applied to the maintenance side of the house.

In 2002, the Office of the Secretary of Defense (OSD) declared that 180 Raptors would suffice but received opposition stating the already decreased amount of 339 would place a strain on U.S. aerial supremacy. The argument stated that without the additional aircraft, funds would instead be redirected to upgrade an aging fleet of F-15s that even following the upgrade would not be capable fighters against new threats. It was later determined the Joint Strike Fighter program's F-35 could assume lighter attack roles relieving the need for additional F/A-22s and lightening the load for F-15s. The total number of F/A-22s ordered dropped to 179 units, though in December of 2005, OSD added production for four additional aircraft bringing the number to 183.

To add additional, yet temporary, concerns air-to-ground testing results showed the aircraft, although capable, would be of better use without assuming the attack role. The DoD decided to revise the aircraft's role to being just that of a fighter platform thus changing the designation from F/A-22 (fighter-attack) to F-22A (fighter only, A model). The F-22A will retain the ability to drop precision guided weaponry, but it will primarily be used for aerial dominance.

In January 2003, F-22A 00-012 was moved from Edwards Air Force Base, California, to Nellis Air Force Base near Las Vegas, Nevada, to begin the integration process to active duty service. Working with the aircraft was the 57th Wing's 57th Aircraft Maintenance Squadron and the 53rd Wing's 422nd Test and Evaluation Squadron.

As was done some thirty years earlier with the F-15A, Langley Air Force Base's 1st Fighter Wing received the first operational F-22A Raptor assigned to the 27th Fighter Squadron on May 12, 2005. Assuming the honors was Lt. Col. James Hecker flying the first of twenty-four freshly painted Raptors from Lockheed Martin's Marietta, Georgia, assembly plant. A few months later on December 15, 2005, the USAF announced the Raptor had reached IOC.

Protecting the Northern Pacific front, Elmendorf, Alaska, was the first combat unit tasked with flying combat sorties by receiving their thirty-six Raptors in the fall of 2007. Members of the 27th Fighter Squadron at Langley brought their F-22As to Elmendorf on May 23, 2006, in support of Exercise Northern Edge to train pilots and maintainers in the cold northwest. First to serve was Raptor 4087.

Although the F-15C will most likely continue to serve until at least 2018, if not longer, the drawdown process had already begun with the arrival of F-22s at Langley Air Force Base. As F-22s would enter their squadron and become combat ready, a process known as beddown, F-15Cs would be removed in equivalent numbers until a full squadron of twenty-four primary aircraft inventory and four backup aircraft inventory numbers were in place.

On November 2, 2007, an F-15 flown by Maj. Stephen Stilwell turned the tides enforcing the need for an F-15 replacement aircraft. Although the F-22 program was well underway and units were already in service, airframe fatigue on the aging Eagles became abruptly apparent. The following is an excerpt from the official 996-page USAF Aircraft Investigation Board Report:

EXECUTIVE SUMMARY
AIRCRAFT ACCIDENT INVESTIGATION
F-15C, T/N 80-0034
LAMBERT FIELD lAP, MISSOURI
2 NOVEMBER 2007

On 2 November 2007, at 0950 Central Standard Time (CST), four F-15C Eagle aircraft departed Lambert Field International Airport (Lambert Field TAP), St. Louis, Missouri (MO) to conduct an air-to-air training mission. At approximately 1011 CST, one of the F-15 aircraft, tail number 80-0034, broke apart in flight and impacted the ground in a wooded area approximately 4 miles south-southeast of Boss, MO; approximately 90 miles south-southwest of Lambert Field IAP. Despite injury to his left shoulder and arm caused by the in-flight breakup, the mishap pilot (MP) ejected successfully and parachuted to the ground. The MP was recovered by local rescue personnel and transported via Life Flight to a St. Louis-area hospital for medical treatment. The mishap aircraft (MA) was based at Lambert Field TAP and assigned to the 110th Fighter Squadron, of the 131st Fighter Wing. The mishap mission was flown in the Lindbergh and Salem Military Operating Areas (MOAs). Lindbergh and Salem MOAs are above predominately agricultural land and forest located approximately 70-150 miles to the southwest of St. Louis, MO. The MA was destroyed upon impact, and the resultant wreckage caused minimal damage to private property.

The mishap flight's mission was to conduct Basic Fighter Maneuvers involving one-on-one offensive attack and defensive

Tail number 80-006

CRACK

The USAF immediately grounded all F-15A-Ds following the crash of 80-0034. Inspection revealed cracks on three aircraft, all containing significant actual flight hours. Aircrafts 80-0006 of the 2nd, 80-0021 of the 34th, and 78-0523 of the 86th Tactical Fighter Squadrons had amassed 6,023, 5,967, and 6,450 flight hours, respectively. Fortunately, none of the cracks had crossed into the main flanges of the longeron. Pictured here are the cracks on 80-0006. *USAF*

Flying in formation with the historic P-51 Mustang and the state-of-the-art F-22 Raptor, the F-15 has undoubtedly found its place in history as one of the greatest fighters ever built and will continue to serve for decades to come. Sandy McDonnell wisely chose to name a new generation of aircraft after the embodiment of the American spirit, the Eagle. *Tyson V. Rininger*

maneuvering. During the MP's second engagement, he maneuvered in a nearly level right-hand turn at approximately 450 knots. With less than 7.8 times the force of gravity (G) loaded upon the aircraft, the MA began shaking violently side to side. The MP then transmitted, "Mick 2, knock it off," while simultaneously rolling wings level and reducing to 1.5 Gs. Within seconds the forward fuselage broke apart from the aft portion of the MA. The MP successfully ejected after the in-flight break-up.

The accident investigation board president found, by clear and convincing evidence, the cause of this accident was a failure of the upper right longeron, a critical support structure in the F-15C aircraft. The MA upper longeron failed to meet blueprint specifications increasing localized stress in the thin web and leading to crack initiation. Engineering and metallurgy analysis of the recovered MA wreckage identified a fatigue crack in the thin web of the longeron near canted fuselage station (CFS) 377 which grew under cyclical flight loads and ultimately led to longeron failure. The longeron failure subsequently triggered a catastrophic failure of the remaining support structures and caused the aircraft to break apart in-flight.

All F-15A-D aircraft were indefinitely grounded pending inspection of the troubled longerons. With tensions in the Middle East, timing couldn't be worse. The F-16 force as well as the Strike Eagles still flying picked up much of the Eagle's workload.

Within the first few weeks, three additional aircraft were found containing cracks in the longerons though they had not yet spread to the main flange portion where they would have most certainly would have failed.

In the months that followed, Eagles slowly returned to the skies reassuming their aerial supremacy roles, though a total of seven aircraft would remain on the ground with longeron fractures. Though support of the F-22 had grown, the fatigue-induced incident only reinforced the justification for replacement of the F-15 Eagle.

Meanwhile, the F-15E Strike Eagle continued to prove its place in the USAF inventory by maintaining vigilance in the Middle East. At this point, there is no practical replacement in store for the Strike Eagle, though specifications regarding an F/B-22 bomber version of the Raptor have been under discussion. The revised bomber variant would feature a larger delta-like wing replacing the need for stabilators increasing the internal fuel capacity resulting in longer range and increased payload.

Due to base realignment and closure studies conducted in the Quadrennial Defense Review, Eagles will soar on providing a high-low mix to the combat arena. Based on age and airframe time, 178 Golden Eagles will be chosen to continue service with the USAF in cooperation with the F-22. Structural upgrades including reinforced weapons stations, vertical tail reconstruction, and flight control upgrades are all expected to take place beginning in 2008. These upgrades are expected to take the Eagle to at least 2025. The remaining 200 F-15s not chosen for the Golden Eagle program are expected to be retired at a rate of twenty per year.

ACKNOWLEDGMENTS

I'll be the first to admit I'm a photographer, not a writer. It is with great humility the majority of images gracing these pages are not my own, but rather of those serving with the U.S. armed forces. It is however with great honor I have the privilege of using these images to illustrate the history of such a great aircraft. Instead of viewing this aircraft from a purely artistic perspective, images provided by our servicemen and women should allow for a more accurate portrayal.

A civilian expert on the F-15, Steve Davies, allowed me to nag him continuously when it came to finding the answers about an aircraft I was formerly unfamiliar with. His co-authored book *F-15 Eagle Engaged* enabled me to verify research information and maintain historical accuracy. It is because of his time and energy, along with his great fascination for this aircraft, that I was able to assemble this publication. Additional thanks goes to Lt. Col. Craig J. Teft, USAF (Ret), a former F-15 pilot, for spreading the word among other Eagle drivers regarding assistance toward the completion of this project.

The "Eagle" wouldn't be nearly as potent without the weapon systems it carries into battle. Good friend Ed Thomas from Raytheon Systems, as well as Everett Tackett, Vito Covalucci, and Jim Muntz, were all great support in acquiring graphics and weapon systems information detailed throughout the book. Without them, I'm pretty certain I'd be missing a chapter!

Starbucks, East Village, Café Noir, various airlines and hotels are all owed a small debt of gratitude for allowing me to camp out and type away for hours among ever-changing environments. Due to the extreme travel necessary for my photography business, other businesses came to the rescue. While not much travel was done as a direct result of this book, its contents were created all over the country. From Prunedale, California, where Lexie, the perky barista, insured I had plenty of coffee, to Susan at MCAS Kaneohe Bay, Hawaii, who was constantly fixing the O'Club's Internet access, I couldn't have done this without them.

While certain establishments assisted with placement, it was my friends who put up with my annoyances. My publisher Steve Gansen calmly dealt with the delays while my "Aerotard" family endured my bickering. (Not about my publisher of course . . . seriously!) My girlfriend, Leticia, patiently put up with my occasional absence while my family came close to placing my photo on milk cartons . . . repeatedly. Thank you all for having faith that I would one day reappear from the stupor that is my computer monitor.

There are many others deserving my thanks, and I'm sure they know who they are. Without you all, this never would have come to fruition. I hope everyone can see the value of their contributions throughout these pages. Many thanks.

GLOSSARY OF ACRONYMS

AFSC: Air Force Strategic Command

AGM: air-to-ground missile

AIM: air intercept missile

AMRAAM: advanced medium range air-to-air missile

ATC: Air Training Command (later, Air Education and
    Training Command)

ATEGG: advanced turbine engine gas generator

AWAC: airborne warning and control system

BLU: bomb live unit

CAP: combat air patrol

CAS: control augmentation system

CBU: cluster bomb unit

CFT: conformal fuel tanks

DoD: Department of Defense

ECM: electronic countermeasure

FFAR: folding fin aerial rockets

GBU: guided bomb unit

GCS: guidance and control section

GPS: global positioning system

GWOT: global war on terrorism

HOTAS: hands-on throttle and stick

HUD: heads-up display

IADS: Iraqi Air Defense System, or Integrated Air Defense System

ICBM: intercontinental ballistic missile

IOC: initial operational capability

ITAG: inertial terrain-aided guidance

JASSM: joint air-to-surface standoff missile

JSOW: joint standoff weapon

LANTIRN: low-altitude navigation and targeting infrared for night

LDGP: low drag general purpose

MSIP: multi-stage improvement program

NFZ: no-fly zone

ONW: Operation Northern Watch

OEF: Operation Enduring Freedom

OSW: Operation Southern Watch

PACAF: Pacific Air Force

RFG: Federal Republic of Germany

SAC: Strategic Air Command

SAM: surface-to-air missile

TAC: Tactical Air Command

TAF: Tactical Air Force

TEWS: tactical electronic warfare suite

TFX: tactical fighter experimental

UAE: United Arab Emirates

USAF: United States Air Force

USN: United States Navy

VG: variable geometry

WCMD: wind-corrected munition dispensers

WCU: weapons control unit

WDU: weapons detonation unit

WGU: weapons guidance unit

WMD: weapons of mass destruction

WSO: weapons safety officer, or weapons system officer

INDEX

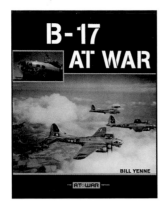
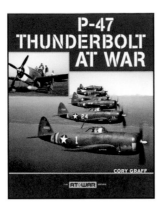
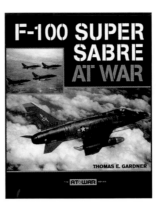
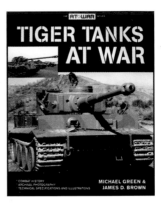

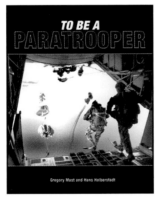

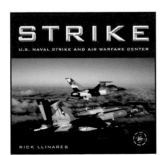
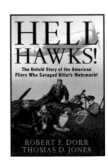